The Mob
and The Mayor

Persecution of the Salvation Army at the Victorian seaside

T0341451

Eastbourne Salvation Army Band, 1891.

This book is dedicated to
the brave and faithful soldiers of the
Eastbourne Salvation Army who marched with music.

The Mob
and The Mayor

Persecution of the Salvation Army at the Victorian seaside

Stephen Huggins

sussex
ACADEMIC
PRESS

Brighton • Chicago • Toronto

2 4 6 8 10 9 7 5 3 1

First published in Great Britain in 2020 by
SUSSEX ACADEMIC PRESS
PO Box 139, Eastbourne BN24 9BP

Distributed in North America by
SUSSEX ACADEMIC PRESS
Independent Publishers Group
814 N. Franklin Street
Chicago, IL 60610

British Library Cataloguing in Publication Data
A CIP catalogue record for this book is available from the British Library.

Library of Congress Cataloging-in-Publication Data
To be applied For.

Paperback ISBN 978-1-78976-084-2

Typeset and designed by Sussex Academic Press, Brighton & Eastbourne.
Printed and bound by CPI Group (UK) Ltd, Croydon, CR0 4YY

CONTENTS

ACKNOWLEDGMENTS

I should like to acknowledge my thanks for the kind help received from Major Ivan Oliver and Major Nigel Bovey of the Salvation Army, Steven Spencer, Director of the Salvation Army International Heritage Centre, London, the East Sussex Records Office and the British Newspaper Archive.

THE ILLUSTRATIONS

The Cover

FRONT: Salvation Army Open-air Meeting. From *'Le Petit Journal'*, 1892.
www.salvationarmy.org.uk/about-us/international-heritage-centre/international-heritage-centre-blog/blood-fire-skulls
Reproduced with permission from The Salvation Army International Heritage Centre.

BACK: Photograph: Alderman Morrison, Mayor of Eastbourne, 1889, courtesy of The Hart Family. H. Hart, via Ancestry.
Reproduced with permission from Henry Hart.

Frontispiece

Photograph: Eastbourne Band, *Marching with Music* pamphlet, Salvation Army International Heritage Centre.
Reproduced with permission from The Salvation Army International Heritage Centre.
Eastbourne Salvation Army Band, 1891.

Map

Eastbourne
Ward Lock & Co's *Illustrated Guide Book Eastbourne, Pevensey, Seaford and District*, Tenth Edition Revised (1933–4), John Bartholomew and Son, Edinburgh.

Epigraph

Line drawing: Louisa Clark (in prison uniform) from journal *All the World*, February 1892.
www.salvationarmy.org.uk/about-us/international-heritage-centre/international-heritage-centre-resources
Reproduced with permission from The Salvation Army International Heritage Centre.

Text

Line drawing: Eastbourne mob attack on the Citadel, The Salvation Army International Heritage Centre.
sahpa.blogspot.com/2011/08/skeleton-army.html
Reproduced with permission from The Salvation Army International Heritage Centre.

Photograph: Eyewitness Story, Bandsman Walter Guy.
www.salvationarmy.org.uk/about-us/international-heritage-centre/international-heritage-centre-resources
Reproduced with permission from The Salvation Army International Heritage Centre.

Photograph taken by the author at the Salvation Army

www.salvationarmy.org.uk/about-us/international-heritage-centre/international-heritage-centre-resources
Reproduced with permission from The Salvation Army International Heritage Centre.

Line drawing: A Welcome outside Lewes Jail, Salvation Army International Heritage Centre.
Reproduced with permission from The Salvation Army International Heritage Centre.

Photograph taken by the author at the Salvation Army Eastbourne Citadel: Battered Bugle.
www.salvationarmy.org.uk/eastbourne-citadel

Reproduced with permission from The Salvation Army Eastbourne Citadel and the South East Division of The Salvation Army.

Photograph taken by the author at the Salvation Army Eastbourne Citadel: Commemorative Wall Plaque.

www.salvationarmy.org.uk/eastbourne-citadel

Reproduced with permission from The Salvation Army Eastbourne Citadel and the South East Division of The Salvation Army.

The Author and Press have made every effort to identify, locate and contact all rightsholders before publication. If we are notified of any omissions or mistakes, the publisher will revise these at the earliest opportunity.

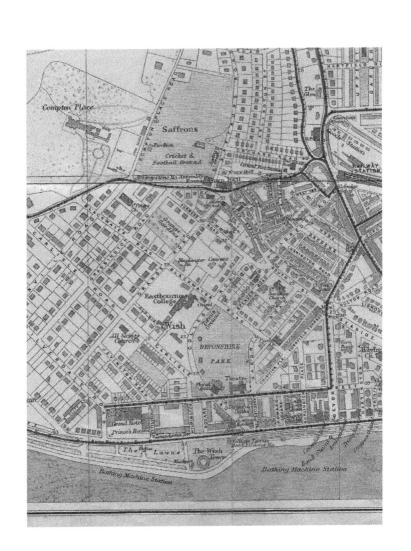

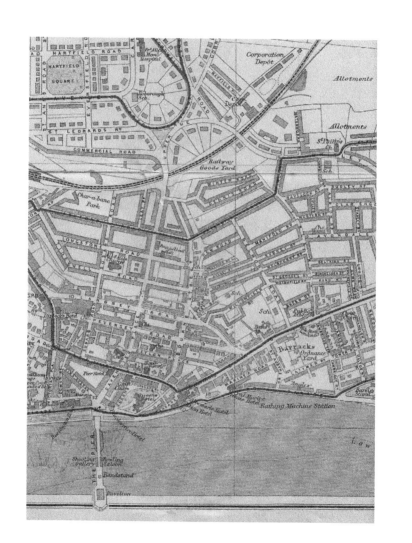

Louisa Clark in her Lewes Prison clothing

Dislike is not a proper ground for legislation . . . When dislike crystallises into a clause in a statute it becomes legislative persecution, and in this case it becomes persecution of the worst kind — religious persecution.

Mr Pember Q.C. before the Select Committee of the House of Lords on the Eastbourne Improvement Act, 1885, Amendment Bill.

A WIDER HISTORY

The Salvation Army has long been a feature of British towns and cities, making a rich and valuable contribution to the life of the nation. The Army is well known for its work with the poor and disadvantaged. Through the work of Salvationists the homeless are given shelter and the addicted are offered rehabilitation. They deliver a wide range of services for the elderly and support those with special needs. Salvationist chaplains regularly visit those in prison and provide support for families. The Army has provided a family tracing service since 1885. Salvation Army mobile emergency units even attend major disaster incidents. In two world wars, Salvationists bravely supported front line troops providing sustenance and an encouraging word.

There is, however, much more to the story of the Salvation Army than their highly commendable good works. It is as if they have been so closely identified with a well regarded programme of social action that their wider history has been either marginalised or ignored. This history includes a period of astonishing levels of opposition which met the Army in its early years. Many Salvationists were badly injured in violent street riots against them while, at the same time, they faced imprisonment for their attempts at evangelism as the force of the law was brought to bear.

It was an extraordinary episode in the history of the Salvation Army and, indeed, for the communities in which it occurred. As such, it richly deserves consideration for it raises very significant questions about both the Salvation Army and the society from which it came.

What went on was no less than religious persecution. It will be important, therefore, to understand what brought the Army and its opponents to this crisis for unless this is considered no real sense can be made of the shocking confrontation. Without putting these matters into an historical context they might simply be regarded as senseless violence born of cruel and hateful prejudice.

Others have already looked at the persecution of the Salvation Army in this period. For example, more than forty years ago Bailey (1977) considered events in a number of provincial towns, Briggs (1981) then looked at the experience of some Sussex towns, Hare (1988) concentrated on events in Worthing and Smith (1990) focussed on the disturbances in Whitchurch. Murdoch (1992) wrote on the clashes between the Salvation Army and Irish Roman Catholics in Liverpool. More recently, Bovey (2015) has presented a very comprehensive chronological account of developments at a national level and Kneale (2018) has made an examination of the situation in Torquay.

Among all those places where the Salvation Army was persecuted that in Eastbourne during the 1880s and 1890s stands out as worthy of attention. The Sussex seaside resort played a hugely important part in the wider anti-Salvation Army narrative as it was here that opposition was among the most violent and protracted and was, significantly and surprisingly, supported by the local Mayor.

At the Salvation Army Citadel in Eastbourne, Langney Road, next to a tattered banner, there is a plaque with this inscription

1891 – The Inner History of the Eastbourne Riots and the fight for liberty to march the streets of Eastbourne accompanied by instrumental music.

Eastbourne mob attack on the Citadel

It refers to a time when to emerge from that same building with the intention of marching through the surrounding streets accompanied by a brass band was to be confronted by an angry, abusive and violent mob of several thousand rioters, aided and abetted by the town Mayor.

This is the story of the brave men and women of the Salvation Army in Eastbourne.

CHAPTER ONE

WILLIAM BOOTH, THE SALVATION ARMY AND THE URBAN POOR

From its very beginning in the nineteenth century the Salvation Army has had a heart for, and mission to, the urban poor. There was good reason for this imperative.

Life for those whose homes were in the slums was unremittingly grim. Their housing was poor and overcrowded, their diets were inadequate and their health almost entirely unchecked. Filth abounded and disease was rampant. Such work as could be found was very often only casual in nature and had no sense of security. Crime rates were high and often linked with the abuse of alcohol and violence. Prostitution was widespread. Not surprisingly the infant mortality rate among the poor was high and general life expectancy low.

The poor lived in well defined, identifiable slum areas of cities, separate from other neighbourhoods. Such places were regarded with fear and revulsion by those on the outside and to be avoided at all costs. Arthur Morrison, the journalist and author, described the slums of Whitechapel in London as

A horrible black labyrinth . . . reeking from end to end with the vilest exhalations; its streets, mere kennels of horrent putrefaction; its every wall, its every object, slimy with the indigenous

ooze of the place; swarming with human vermin, whose trade is robbery, and whose recreation is murder; the catacombs of London – darker, more tortuous and more dangerous than those of Rome, and supersaturated with foul life . . . Outcast London. Black and nasty still, a wilderness of crazy dens into which pallid wastrels crawl to die; where several families lie in each fetid room, and fathers, mothers and children watch each other starve; where bony, bleary-eyed wretches, with everything beautiful, brave, and worthy crushed out of them, and nothing of the glory and nobleness and jollity of this world within range of their crippled senses, rasp away their puny lives in the sty of the sweater.[1]

The terrible living conditions of the slums were widely held to be both the cause and the product of the spiritual and moral corruption of the inhabitants. A Salford clergyman, commenting on local industrial development, argued that it had

. . . drawn together a most heterogenous population, consisting in no small degree, of the unsettled, the discontented and the depraved; so as to render our trading districts . . . the moral sewers of the community – a confluence of the scum and the offscouring of society.[2]

The rapid and massive growth in towns and cities had meant that many churches were ill-equipped to minister within them. The Church of England lacked a parish system which was capable of meeting the needs of the emerging urban areas, while many of their clergy were from upper and middle-class backgrounds and lacking in understanding of life in the slums. The Nonconformist churches were in a similarly difficult position. Methodism emphasised industry, thrift and, above all, respectability which, together with their adoption of the Anglican practice of pew rents, excluded the poor, wittingly or not. The Baptists were not primarily located in urban areas while the Congregationalists often focussed their work more on the middle classes. The emphasis for the Roman Catholic Church at this time tended to centre on the need to retain its membership rather than extension.

This is not to suggest that the various churches made no attempts to reach out to the poor for there were notable examples of such work going on in city slums throughout much of the second half of the century.[3] However, what is being proposed is, in a wider sense, given the enormity of the numbers of people involved, and the sheer depth of the poverty in which they were forced to live, that there was insufficient work in the slums which was co-ordinated, resourced and sustained by the churches and that the work which did go on by and large lacked any degree of any lasting success.

There were those who were very critical of the churches for their lack of concern towards the poor. One of these was William Booth who was to go on to found and lead the Salvation Army. Affronted by what he saw as the indolence and indifference of the churches in this matter William earnestly believed that it was the duty of all Christians, and especially those appointed ministers among them, to be active in going to the poor who needed to be converted and saved.

The future General Booth had received very little by the way of formal education or ministerial training. Even his beloved wife, Catherine, a woman of quite some intellectual substance, could not persuade him to embrace scholarship.

Notwithstanding this perceived shortcoming Booth was convinced that he was chosen and called to work with the poor. He said

> . . . I feel it in my heart – on my soul from day to day that I would be a missionary of God.[4]

As a Bible literalist William believed that hell and eternal damnation awaited all those who had not found salvation and was firmly convinced that all people should be warned of what awaited them. If the established churches would not go to the slums with this message then he must do so. Many were attracted to share this passionate calling believing that any personal sacrifice was worth paying in order to bring the Christian message to the poor.

In 1859 a religious revival began which spread across the country and William, together with his new wife, Catherine, toured as independent evangelists. By the mid-1860s the couple felt called to minister in London's East End amongst the poorest in the capital and so he was pleased to accept an invitation from the publishers of the weekly evangelical *Revival* to take up a three-week preaching engagement for them in Whitechapel. William preached in the teeming streets and even held services in a tent set up in a Quaker burial ground in order to attract people. Through his passion, oratory and singular methods between four and five hundred of the local poor came to take part in his services.

William now felt especially called to focus his work in the East End.

> *In every direction were multitudes totally ignorant of the gospel, and given up to all kinds of wickedness – infidels, drunkards, thieves, harlots, gamblers, blasphemers, and pleasure seekers without number . . . A voice seemed to sound in my ears, "Why go . . . anywhere else, to find souls that need the Gospel? Preach to them, the unsearchable riches of Christ. I will help you – your need will be supplied.*[5]

The work continued apace with more open air preaching together with well attended gatherings held in various rented accommodation. William formed the East London Revival Society which was soon renamed as the East London Christian Mission. He continued to feel that it was here among the poorest that he had found his calling.

. . . I was continually haunted with a desire to offer myself to Jesus Christ as an apostle for the heathen of East London. The idea, or heavenly vision, or whatever you may call it overcame me. I yielded to it, and what has happened since is I think not only a justification but an evidence that my offer was accepted.[6]

The work of the Christian Mission met with much success and within a short while William felt that he must expand his work first to other parts of London and then to the provinces. This move was also successful and brought about a further renaming to reflect the new and wider scope of his mission and so in 1878 the name Salvation Army came to be. Its growth and spread were to be rapid.

The religious landscape of Britain was about to be changed but not first without a significant degree of courage, sacrifice and, above all, faith on the part of Booth and his newly formed Salvation Army.

1   Morrison, *The Palace Journal*, April 24 1889, p. 1022.
2   August (2007), *The British Working Class, 1832–1940*, Pearson Longman, p. 9.
3   For example, within the Church of England the Anglo Catholic 'slum priests' served with distinction while the Settlement Movement, such as at Toynbee Hall, made encouraging efforts to bring the social classes together. The work of the Methodist West London Mission was also significant in this area.
4   Sandall (1947), *The History of the Salvation Army, Volume One, 1865–1878*, Thomas Nelson & Sons, p. 6.
5   *The East London Evangelist*, October 1868, p. 3.
6   Railton (1889), *Twenty one years' Salvation Army: Under the generalship of William Booth*, The Salvation Army Publishing Offices, p. 19.

CHAPTER TWO

VICTORIAN RESPONSES TO THE SALVATION ARMY

Within just over a decade of its beginning the Salvation Army had almost fourteen hundred Corps and four and a half thousand full-time officers in the United Kingdom alone.[1] However, as Army membership rose and its work spread they came up against a groundswell of opposition the likes of which had not been experienced in this country for quite some time. It was to result in the arrest of many of its members and the toleration and encouragement by many of the street violence perpetrated on them by angry mobs. The roots of this antipathy towards the Salvation Army were many and varied.

The growth of the Army meant that William Booth soon became a national figure, drawing much public attention. The majority of this was very negative with considerable animus directed towards him, personally. William's eccentric appearance was mocked and he was criticised by sophisticates for being vulgar. He cut the figure of an Old Testament prophet, his language deeply Biblical in both style and content. William was derided as a religious fanatic. He was lampooned and traduced in the press for giving himself the title 'General'. Those with anti-Catholic sentiment accused him of acting like 'Pope Booth' and seeking a second Reformation, while the virulent anti-Semitism of the time was also brought to bear. A local newspaper was not alone in its tone in reporting of the visit of the 'Jew General' to the area in order to draw money from people. T.H. Huxley accused Booth of being a Socialist, describing his proposals for social reform and assistance proposed in the *In Darkest England* Scheme as "Socialism in disguise". Not surprisingly, the vilification that William received soon also attached itself to the movement which he founded and the so-called 'Boothites' became marked men and women.

By the mid-1880s the Salvation Army was already to be found ministering in many poor areas across the country. Other Christian churches became concerned at the progress of their work. The Church of England reacted badly against their co-religionists, especially with what was seen as the uncontrollable emotionalism and lack of due reverence in its worship, professed and distinct anti-clericalism and absence of the sacraments. Many Anglicans were roundly critical of the Army, which they claimed tended towards emotionalism in religion.

Salvationists were keen to use any suitable method to attract people. Their hymns were often set to popular music hall tunes of the day, their sermons were short and were thought by some to lack what was held as a necessary scholarship and the language of prayer was often in the vernacular. Anglicans, nurtured for centuries on the reverent language of the Book of Common Prayer and the King James Bible, responded to Salvationist worship with horror, describing it as being nothing more than closely bordering on irreverence, using shockingly familiar language in prayer and an over excitement in worship which were altogether inexpressibly distasteful.

Salvationists were even accused of encouraging sexual immorality amongst those whom they ministered when it was pointed out that illegitimate births had increased in proportion to the number of meetings which the Salvation Army had held in some parts of the country.

As part of the established order of society, the Church of England saw the Army to comprise a wider social threat. The Dean of Carlisle even argued that it would lead to a subversion of the social system and the uprooting of every Christian church. Nor was the Army well received by some Nonconformists. A Methodist journal suggested that the Army's mission methods were nothing but "wretched accretions and corrupt fungi". Politicians, too, spoke out against the Salvation Army. Lord Shaftesbury, the great social reformer, even associated their work with that of the Devil who, he asserted, used them to make Christianity appear ridiculous.

The Salvation Army also drew a strong and negative reaction from publicans and brewers. Salvationists insisted on a total abstinence from alcohol. On becoming a soldier in the Salvation Army an individual signed the Articles of War, which included a declaration to refrain from the use of all intoxicating liquors. The growth and spread of the Army was seen as a clear threat to the continued high sales of alcohol. It would not do were the poor to be encouraged to temperance. The alcohol trade used its influence with magistrates and local councillors to ensure that vested interests were kept intact. At one time, William Booth wrote to the Home Secretary alleging that

> . . . *in nearly every town where there has been any opposition we have been able to trace it more or less, to the direct instigation, and often open leadership of either Brewers or Publicans, or their EMPLOYEES.*[2]

At the local level drinkers were often bribed with beer by publicans. Booth claimed

> . . . *drunken men are instigated, and bribed with liquor to annoy, and, if possible, break up meetings.*[3]

The alcohol industry was not about to relinquish its access to such a vast market among the poor.

The Salvation Army was also certainly radical in the access it gave women to public Christian ministry. In an age of profound sexual inequality this attracted strenuous opposition. Although William was not, at first, convinced of the position, through the gentle, yet robust, encouragement of his wife, Catherine, he became persuaded that women had an equal right to hold and exercise authority in ministry. Many

evangelical *Revival,* echoed their thoughts:

> *The first woman taught her husband with the tree of knowledge of good and evil; and with a righteous wisdom the Holy Ghost forbids her ever to teach the man again.*[4]

However, as early as 1875 women had been given sole charge of Salvation Army Stations. Just five years later women had come to comprise half of all Salvation Army officers. Women, many of them young and working class, filled the ranks of what became known as the 'Hallelujah Lasses'. Dressed in smart Army uniforms which proclaimed the authority of their work, the Lasses were sent out into the slums as street evangelists. Such contradiction of traditionally ascribed gender roles scandalised many who saw them as disruptive and sensationalist. Their success was remarkable. It was reported in South Wales that they

> *. . . have been the means of drawing hundreds of the lowest classes of people to hear the Gospel preached, people who are undoubtedly beyond the reach of our ministers.*[5]

relations challenged Victorian notions of patriarchy in a fundamental and far reaching way. To many Christians it seemed that the ministry of Salvationist women contradicted the teaching of the Bible. At the same time, in many of the poorer neighbourhoods in which they ministered, the role of Salvation Army women called into question assumptions about male authority, and even notions of masculinity itself. Many Salvation Army women would bravely come to bear an abusive and violent backlash against their ministry.

Opposition to the Salvation Army also arose from within the working-class neighbourhoods in which the Army went about their evangelism. It became quite clear to residents that their whole way of life and sense of place was under attack which, figuratively, it was. This may be seen in the Army method of targeting an area. Posters would be displayed and handbills distributed announcing the Army's intentions. The language used was both sensationalist and distinctly military in nature. Neighbourhoods were depicted as 'battlefields' which were to be 'invaded' and 'prisoners captured'. Uniformed Salvationists would come in numbers into an area to present an identifiable presence. On street corners, outside public houses and anywhere in the open air that it was thought that people would be attracted there would be Salvationists preaching, hymn singing and praying. All this could take place at most times of day and, sometimes, at night as well. The message always unequivocally proclaimed was that people were sinners on their way to hell unless they repented and became a soldier in the Salvation Army. Many were affronted and strongly objected. Feelings could run high and there were often public confrontations between Salvationists and locals. A Manchester newspaper reported a court case arising from an assault on a Salvationist in such a situation.

The complainant said that when leading a procession through the streets (the) defendant assaulted him by pulling his coat collar, and threatened to cut his throat. The defendant said the Salvation Army caused a most disgraceful disturbance in the streets, and on Monday night obscene language was used by those in the procession. Stones and mud were thrown, and the

*captain hurled an umbrella in the defendant's face, but he
pushed it to one side. The Stipendiary (magistrate) said
complainant had failed to make out a case, and he should
dismiss it. The Army appeared to him to cause breaches of the
peace.*[6]

There would be many other much worse incidents to come.

A further major area of contention developed around the
Salvation Army's use of brass bands in their street evangelism.
In 1880 General Booth had issued *Orders for Bands.* In these
he first drew directly on biblical teaching about music in
worship, pointing to Scripture for authority in his plans.[7] The
General then went on to draw up a list of those instruments
which should be used in Army bands.

There were a number of reasons why brass bands came to
be the preferred means to accompany the open air worship
and evangelism of the Army. Brass bands were popular at the
time and enjoyed by many and would attract people to where
Salvationists were evangelising. They were also a practical
response to the noise and bustle of the busy streets, and, when
the situation necessitated, could be used to drown the cries of
ridicule and derision thrown at Salvationists. Indeed, so extensive was the Salvation Army use of brass bands in their
work that they soon became closely identified in the public
imagination.

Many people thoroughly disapproved of what the Army
was doing. Publicans certainly did not want Salvationists
making a 'holy noise' outside their premises. It was also the
case that as the Salvation Army insisted on marching with
music on a Sunday that they attracted even more public
displeasure. At this time many working people only had
Sunday as a day of rest from hard physical labour and they
wished for the peace and quiet in which to enjoy it. There
were many complaints against Salvationists in this matter.
Further, the wider issue of what could or could not be done
on a Sunday was very much alive then. The balance of power

and influence was beginning to pass from those who insisted on the Sabbath being set apart for worship and the quiet of the home to those who looked to liberalise the day. This was a hotly disputed topic in the late nineteenth century and the Salvation Army became deeply embroiled in it. As will be seen this was to be especially the case in Eastbourne where their opponents made marching with music on Sunday a particular focus.

Victorian society did not really know how to respond to the rise of the Salvation Army whose radical approach to Christianity challenged the sense of security and firmly held assumptions of many. As the Salvation Army was so innovative in terms of organisation and method, and was firmly prepared to stand by its principles, many saw it as a threat. As such, opposition grew rapidly with many widely differing interest groups coming together against the Salvationists in an unlikely and toxic coalescence which cut across class and denominational allegiances. From the outset the Salvation Army faced opposition which was bitter, determined and sprang from many sources.

1   It had also successfully spread to several other European countries and to the United States, and as well as parts of the British Empire. Booth (1890), *In darkest England, and the way out,* Funk & Wagnalls, Appendix 1.

2   Quoted in Horridge (2015), *The Salvation Army – Origins and Early Days: 1865–1900,* Abernant Publishing, p. 84.

3   Horridge, *op. cit.,* p. 79.

4   Quoted in Walker (2001), *Pulling the Devil's Kingdom Down,* University of California Press, p.46.

5   *South Wales Daily News,* 15 March 1879.

6   *Manchester Courier, and Lancashire General Advertiser,* 14 January 1880.

7   For example, Psalm 98: 6 – *With trumpets and sound of cornet make a joyful noise before the LORD, the King.* Similarly, Psalm 150 – *Praise him with the sound of the trumpet: praise him with the psaltery and harp. Praise him with the timbrel and dance: praise him with stringed instruments*

and organs. Praise him upon the loud cymbals: praise him upon the high sounding cymbals. Let everything that hath breath praise the Lord. *Praise ye the* Lord.

CHAPTER THREE

EASTBOURNE:
A SEASIDE LIONS' DEN

The Sussex coastal town of Eastbourne was a seemingly unlikely place for some of the worst excesses of the persecution brought to bear on the Salvation Army. There were, however, features of life in the town which added to and compounded the national situation so that Eastbourne became the scene of a ferocious and drawn out struggle between Salvationists and their opponents turning the seaside resort into something of a national *cause célèbre*. It was, a Councillor Wenham put it, as if Eastbourne had become

. . . the cockpit of the fight for religious liberty in this country.[1]

As in many other towns the population of Eastbourne had grown rapidly throughout the nineteenth century. In 1801 it had been estimated at some 1,760 residents and then almost doubled to around 3,400 in the next fifty years. By 1881 the population had then further increased dramatically to just over 22,000.

Those many who came to live in the town were drawn largely from two quite distinct social groups. The Eastbourne authorities set out to attract those from relatively well-off professional and middle-class backgrounds who would look to the town as a suitably quiet place for retirement. The population was further increased by working-class people drawn from across Sussex, many from Lewes, who were in search of employment.

Both groups had keenly felt reason to oppose the Salvation Army. Those from among the better off who had retired to the town would have found the Salvationist commitment to the poor and their unorthodox evangelistic methods towards them as quite alien. The association between the Salvation Army and the poor was sufficient, in itself, for them to be regarded as anathema. The arrival of the Salvation Army in the town would do nothing to enhance the peace and quiet which had brought them to Eastbourne. As such they would have had no natural sympathy for the Army. Meanwhile the working-class incomers who had moved from Lewes brought with them a tradition of independence and determined opposition to authority which are clearly expressed in the pronounced defiant and irreverent ribaldry of their cherished 5th of November Bonfire Night celebrations.

It was also the case that the Eastbourne authorities used a planned development to accommodate the housing needs of the growing town which acted to create a social climate in which antipathy between the social classes would flourish and grow. The authorities based their plans on an openly expressed desire to develop different areas of the town for these different social classes of residents. George Wallis, agent for the Devonshire family of local landowners accurately observed that

> . . . there would be the extension of good large houses in one direction; and there would be the extension of smaller houses in another direction; and they are not mixed up. We have what we call our artisan town; we have our high class villa town; and we have our terraced houses; and they are all quite separate.[2]

Divided by the central commercial and entertainment area, the affluent in the west were kept separate from the poor in the eastern neighbourhoods of the town. Two hotels marked the boundaries, with the Grand at the western end marking off the central commercial, leisure and entertainment district from the Meads, while the working-class neighbourhoods at the eastern end were demarked by the Queen's Hotel close to the pier. The natural outcome of this social engineering was that there was little by way of contact or interaction between the classes other than that necessitated by trade. Writing of these two social groups George Meek put it well:

> *Eastbourne is one of the loveliest pleasure towns in England. It is the paradise of the idle and sometimes vicious rich, the rest-place of the jaded well-paid workers; but it is hell to the poor who try to live in it by casual labour.*[3]

The increase in population put pressure on local services and amenities. This included access to church going. Only some thirty years before there had been sufficient church buildings to accommodate the vast majority of worshippers but this was no longer the case.[4] The response was for more church buildings to be put up. Reflecting on this some many years later Councillor George Chambers observed,

> *. . . East-bourne was growing rapidly; more church accommodation was an increasingly-urgent need.*[5]

However, whether by intent or not, the classes were largely kept apart in their church going. Anglican building development was predominately located in the south western and

(1878–80) in Carlisle Road, St John's (1868–69) in St John's Road, St Peter's (1894–96) in Meads Road, St Saviour's (1867–68) in South Street and St Anne's (1880) in Upperton Gardens were all built.[6] In the poorer more populous eastern end of the town there was an Anglican mission church provided by a richer parish. Christ Church (1859), in Seaside had originally been a Chapel of Ease for Holy Trinity, in Trinity Trees near to the town centre and continued to be so until 1864. However, given the population numbers in the

area there was not so much by way of further Anglican church
building not withstanding that at All Souls, (1879–82), in
Susan's Road.

Nonconformist churches were certainly to be found in the
east. These included the Wesleyan Methodist Chapel (1864)
in Pevensey Road, Beamsley Primitive Methodist Chapel
(1886) in Beamsley Road, the Calvinistic Independent
Chapel (1857) in Cavendish Place, Baptist Church (1871) in
Ceylon Place and the Congregational Church (1862) in
Pevensey Road.[7] There were also several Mission Halls in the
area. In addition to a briefly lived Mission Hall in Leslie Street
two others stand out. Leaf Hall (1864) in Pevensey Road had
been built with the intention of promoting the social, moral
and spiritual welfare of the working classes of Eastbourne. The
Hall had strong links with local temperance groups including
the Band of Hope. Perhaps for this reason it was vandalised
on a number of occasions by those who resented their work?

The other mission presence was that of Longstone Hall in
Longstone Road. An evangelical group came together in the
hall for what were described as 'Full Salvation and Holiness
Meetings'. They were certainly active meeting for worship
and fellowship four times on Sundays and a further three
during the week. The hall also functioned as a soup kitchen
for the local poor and needy. A small number of Salvationists
were attracted to and took part in the worship at the Hall. In
a letter to a local newspaper a Mr Gill who had lead the Whit
Monday services there noted that

> There were some Salvation Army people in the congregation
> . . . and that . . . a mob of drunken roughs assembled outside
> the building, some of whom forced their way in, bent on
> disturbance . . . [8]

The use of Longstone Hall was later loaned to the Salvation
Army for their own worship. As a result, in the public percep-
tion there was a clear association between the regular hall users

and the Army. Miss S. Bell, who was responsible for the hall and well known locally for her interest in mission work, wrote to the press to make clear the distinction between the two groups. While she welcomed the Salvation Army she wrote:

> *Although we work on their lines, the absence of the uniform, flags etc., is sufficient to prove this fact.*[9]

When the Salvation Army began to increase their presence and activity in the town, Miss Bell felt the need to write to the newspaper again in the following year. She said that the regular worshippers at Longstone Hall

> *. . . were in no way identified with the Salvation Army . . . but . . . simply local men and women, who have themselves known the curse of sin, and who spent all their leisure time in trying to rescue others . . . and that . . . when the Salvationists came to the town to reside they joined their work, and were welcomed, and this she expected, caused the public to identify them with that body.*[10]

While members of Longstone Hall were clearly sympathetic to the work of the Salvationists the fact that they wished to distinguish themselves from the Army casts an early light on the growing opposition in the town. Despite their best endeavours it was not without good reason that, when the Primitive Methodists later took over the Hall, they described the lack of any long lasting mission success as

> *. . . partly due to the old reputation clinging to Longstone Hall, and partly to the fact that the Hall is situated in the midst of a non-church going, almost anti-church population.*[11]

As may be seen, the working-class communities located in the east end of Eastbourne were not well served by the Church of England and while Nonconformist churches were active in the area it was the case that they had only limited mission success probably due to their emphasis on respectability.

Late Victorian Eastbourne was not only a place in which to live but also one to visit. The town prided itself on having a sense of respectability and genteel tranquillity. It claimed to have the healthiest climate in England and the best waters, styling itself as a select resort. The high self-esteem felt by the town was clearly expressed at the time:

With the improvements which are continually being carried out, there is no reason why the town should not, year by year, increase its present firm hold on London holiday-makers . . . Of the town itself it is unnecessary to say a word, its renown being such that it now enjoys the enviable title of "Empress of Watering Places" . . . it probably at the present time enjoys a patronage, that for influence and extent exceeds anything of which other south coast watering places are able to boast.[12]

Eastbourne developed a thriving tourism industry as people came to enjoy sea bathing, promenading, visiting the pier and town theatres. Most of those first visitors were from middle and upper class backgrounds but this was soon to change.

By the last quarter of the nineteenth century, with changing conditions in some employment sectors, more working-class people were now able to afford to go on holiday. In Eastbourne this coincided with two events which contributed to a wider social range of people being able to visit the town. In 1863 an outbreak of Scarlet Fever in Eastbourne killed many and scared lots of visitors away. As a result hotels and guesthouses were forced to lower their rates with the consequence that the town became more accessible and attractive to those with lower incomes. Four years later Eastbourne was further opened up to a broader range of tourists with the extension of the rail line from the capital down to the town by the London, Brighton & South Coast

Railway. Many more now took advantage of the opportunity to spend time at the seaside.

The arrival of greater numbers of visitors from a wider social background impacted greatly on Eastbourne. Despite much local temperance activity sales of alcohol increased significantly throughout the holiday season which resulted in an increase in incidents of public drunkenness.[13]

The anonymity of a seaside holiday also provided opportunity for sexual adventure among those set free from the usual constraints of Victorian moral expectations. Intent on their personal enjoyment, tourists could pursue a liberated hedonism which challenged and clashed with notions of respectability. As such the Salvation Army had a keen mission interest in what was going on in seaside resorts like Eastbourne and not always with the gratitude of those involved.

Among the many who so fiercely opposed the Salvation Army in Eastbourne two stand out. One was the violent and intimidatory mob known as the Skeleton Army, while the other was Alderman W. E. Morrison, three times Mayor of Eastbourne. Together these would comprise the crucible in which the courage and faith of the Eastbourne Corps of the Salvation Army would be tried.

Between 1881 and 1893 the so-called Skeleton Army constituted the most significant threat to the continued national existence of the Salvation Army. They were to be found in many towns, especially across Southern England. In all there were Skeleton groups to be found in some sixty towns and cities. They were very active along the South Coast all the way from Hastings to Torquay, with Sussex becoming a particularly hard fought battleground.

The Skeleton Army comprised very largely, but not exclusively, of young working-class men who came together to form loosely based neighbourhood street gangs. There was no single, unified Skeleton Army. Court records of those members of the Skeleton Army who were arrested and tried suggest that they shared much of the same class and

The Skeleton Army attack

occupational backgrounds as their Salvationist opponents. It
may well be that individuals were known to one another in
other social contexts and motives for opposition may have
been compounded by other issues. Significantly, there were
known links between the East End of London, where the
Salvation Army had been first opposed, and Brighton and
other South Coast towns. Councillor George Chambers went
so far as to suggest that the East End had some claim on
Eastbourne.

In the Sussex context there appears to be a strong measure
of association between members of the Skeleton Army and
those belonging to local bonfire societies.[14] The two shared a
common anti-authoritarian outlook and purpose. Such was
the degree of similarity in terms of organisation, method and
identity between them it is likely they shared many members
in common. That there were many thriving bonfire societies
in Eastbourne at this time is probably due in part to the

impetus received for this cultural tradition which had been brought by incomers from Lewes.[15]

As elsewhere, the Skeleton Army in Eastbourne opposed Salvationists through the use of a variety of tactics. At one level, parody and ridicule were prominently employed through a method known as 'rough musicing' which was something akin to 'horse play'. As such it was a means through which the Skeletons could show their disapproval of the Salvation Army. Its aim was to bring about the public humiliation of the opponent. So it was that the Skeletons in particular targeted for appropriation and mimicry the features of the Salvation Army which most distinguished them from other groups. Salvationist uniform was a particular issue here. Not only did the Skeletons wear elaborate costumes modelled on the Salvationist uniform but, wherever possible, they would steal or damage their uniform, especially the caps and bonnets, and also musical instruments. The Salvation Army flag was a frequent target for damage and theft. The Skeleton Army flag was itself a parody having the insignia 'Blood and Thunder' to that of the Salvationist 'Blood and Fire'.

The Skeleton Army in Eastbourne would also use much more direct action against Salvationists in terms of physical violence against them. Time and again members of the Eastbourne Corps were punched, kicked, spat upon and had excrement and rotten offal thrown over them.

Walter Guy, a Bandsman member of the Eastbourne Corps, was only 19 at the time of the riots. Although his diary of the events was not written until some years later it does provide a very useful eye witness account of what went on and who was involved. He recorded:

As the tide of opposition grew, the town became a centre with people coming from all directions, some as far as London, from Worthing in the west and Rye in the east, and all the towns and villages in between. They came in thousands to look on and take part in the "fun", and all the rough element from everywhere joined forces with them. They came by road, on bicycles, horse and trap, walking, by rail excursion, anyhow as long as they could get to Eastbourne. Among this crowd were the local characters, one man, tall and heavy bearded, was prominent in his opposition. We nicknamed him "Goatie". His behaviour was bad. At times, as he would lead them on, his language was awful, and his example was very fully followed. The cursing and swearing, boos, hoots, whistles, coupled with flour, rotten eggs, fish gut, rotten fruit and vegetables and many more horrible and dirty things were thrown at us, at times it was dreadful to put up with them, but it did not daunt any. Hats, bonnets and parts of clothes were torn up but there was no slacking off by the soldiers.[16]

The Skeleton Army in Eastbourne drew further on a range of support from those who, though not personally involved in the physical battles with Salvationists, gave much by way of both a tacit consent and a lively barrage of letters of complaint about the Salvation Army to the local press. In this way the young working-class men who formed the majority of the Skeleton Army in effect became the focus and means through which other interest groups could confront the Salvation Army.

There developed both unintentional and decidedly intentional alliances between Skeleton groups and members of the wider community who also regarded the ingress of the Salvation Army to the town as a direct threat to their interests. As Eastbourne had grown as a resort it attracted businessmen, financiers and entrepreneurs all of whom were intent on making money from tourism in the town. Repeated violent riots in the town would do nothing to attract visitors who were intent on making holiday and spending money. Owners of hotels, guest houses and other tourist attractions would potentially face financial difficulty.

The most active in this regard were brewers and publicans. As a growing seaside resort Eastbourne had many places where alcohol was sold and consumed and the work of the Salvation Army was a direct threat to the trade. Many public houses were used as meeting places and recruiting centres for the Skeleton Army. It was rumoured locally that men were brought into Skeleton activity by being bribed with beer. Walter Guy again provides a valuable account of the link between the Skelton Army and public houses in Eastbourne.

> *The public houses were the meeting places where they made and talked over the plans of opposition, and with the afternoon incidents over, they would return and talk over and tell tales about it, and if any of them had got something it was shewn round, and the publican would have it for so much beer. Across the bar there would be a line sketched on which pieces of clothing, parts of instruments, tambourine, pieces of drum, Pocket Bible leaves, and some "spicy pieces" which formed the subject of the talk and the suggestive tales that went the rounds of the bar.*[17]

The Skeleton Army lacked any measured degree of cohesion and organisation, there being no one overall Army as such. Indeed, some towns had more than one Army, such as in nearby Hastings. However, local Skeleton groups in Sussex could rely on one another for support in their fight against the Salvation Army in a particular town and at a particular time. This is well illustrated in a report on the riots at Eastbourne from a Midlands newspaper:

> *A correspondent states that roughs from Worthing and Hastings joined in Sunday night's disturbance, and the police were at times powerless. The branches of the Skeleton Army in the various Sussex towns are in regular communication.*[18]

In the case of the Skeletons in Eastbourne they were also able to find support for their opposition to the Salvation Army from an unlikely source in the person of the town Mayor.

William Epps Morrison was originally from Glasgow though before coming to Eastbourne in 1878 had lived and worked in Palermo, Italy. The family had considered a return to Scotland but opted for the South Coast because the climate was felt more suitable for the delicate health of his wife, Alexandrina. Mayor Morrison was held in high regard by many of his fellow townsmen, being elected to the office in three consecutive years, 1889–92. Kindness and charity were his hallmark. He was well known to give generously in support of needy individuals who approached him personally and to the wider community. A newspaper account of his funeral in 1895 noted that

> *he was a steadfast and generous supporter of almost every useful and philanthropic society in the town . . . Mr Morrison must have spent no inconsiderable portion of his means on works of charity.*[19]

Mayor Morrison was very involved in helping many local clubs and societies to develop.[20] He was a devout Christian, worshipping at St Saviour's Parish Church in South Street where he was a Sidesman. The Mayor was also very actively involved with the Freemasons being associated with several local lodges and rising to become Senior Provincial Grand Warden of Sussex Freemasons. There can be little doubt that Mayor Morrison made a significant contribution to life in Eastbourne. Albeit from an essentially patrician position he took part in and gave of much of himself to the community. Indeed, such was the volume and strain of this work that he died in December 1895 aged 52 only a little while after stepping down from public office.

Unfortunately, there was another side to Mayor Morrison which seems at odds with many other aspects of his life. Not that he is singular in this regard. People are often very complicated and their actions simply a reflection of complex and unresolved issues. However, there can be no doubt that while the Salvation Army would still have been opposed in Eastbourne as they were in many other towns and cities that it was the driving and forceful vehemence brought by Mayor Morrison that escalated and prolonged the crisis in this particular location.

In 1885 the Eastbourne Improvement Act Clause 169 had forbidden public processions in the town on Sundays when accompanied by music. The Salvation Army took the view that these formed a vital component in their street evangelism to the poor and they were quite prepared to be disobedient on the matter whatever the consequences. Mayor Morrison always maintained that he had no issue with the Salvation Army except where they actually broke the law. He said

> *We have attempted from the very first to eliminate any sort of discussion as to what the Salvation Army is or is not . . . The only question that has come before us has been with regard to maintaining the law and nothing else.*[21]

The truth may be seen to lay elsewhere as before taking up the office of Mayor he had said that the Eastbourne Town Council should do all it could

> *. . . to put down the Salvation Army business which was opposed altogether to the spirit of the town.*[22]

What it was that moved a man so committed to serving the public good as Mayor Morrison to have such ill-feeling towards his fellow Christians is not easy to comprehend. What drove him to act in the extraordinary way that he did towards the Salvation Army and to abuse the office of mayor in doing so? There may have been a number of possible reasons. Was it that, in the context of late nineteenth century class relations and from his upper middle-class position, he took exception both to the essentially working-class nature and ethos of the Army and those whom they sought to evangelise? Given that the mayor took a lead in the situation may it have been that he found it unacceptable that his own authority was so directly challenged and called into question? May it have been he felt that the impact the Salvation Army and the associated riots in the town were damaging to the reputation and future prosperity of the Eastbourne? Was it simply he was a bigot and a bully who abused the power and authority of his office?

Whatever Mayor Morrison's motives in his dealings with the Salvation Army his antipathy towards them is startlingly clear. More than any other individual, Mayor Morrison was responsible for the violent persecution of the Salvation Army which went on in the town. He both set the tone and took an active part in proceedings.

It is hard to consider that the story which now follows occurred on the South Coast, in the Sussex seaside resort of Eastbourne, only some one hundred and thirty years ago.

1   *Eastbourne Gazette,* 29 November 1891.

2   Griggs (2016), *Eastbourne 1851–1951: A Social History,* Grosvenor House Publishing, p. 13.

3   Quoted in Neville (1982), *Religion and Society in Eastbourne, 1735–1920,* Eastbourne Local History Society, p. 12.

4   Census returns show that at a time when the population of Eastbourne was a little under eight and a half thousand there were twenty one places of worship, comprising fifteen Anglican and six Nonconformist churches. Vickers (1989), *The Religious Census of Sussex,* Sussex Record Society, p. 28.

5   Chambers (1910), *East Bourne Memories,* Sumfield, p. 185.

6   Interestingly, at St Anne's the practice of pew rentals was only abandoned in 1943 when it was finally recognised as ' . . . an out of date system'. *Eastbourne Gazette,* 27 March 1943.

7   The Congregationalists attempted a form of mission to the unchurched of the area through their Pleasant Sunday Afternoon Brotherhood. It was, as its name implies, an attempt to engage with the altogether brief leisure time of working-class men. The P.S.A.B. was essentially the product of the Nonconformist churches. It was viewed with suspicion by some who felt that it

was lacking in reverent observation of the Sabbath while others went still further describing its supporters as ' . . . direct agents of secularization' *Bolton Chronicle,* 3 November 1888.

8 *Eastbourne Gazette,* 23 May 1883.

9 *Eastbourne Gazette,* 11 April 1883.

10 *Eastbourne Gazette,* 5 November 1884.

11 Neville, *op. cit.,* p. 17.

12 *Eastbourne Gazette,* 15 January 1890.

13 For example, the Eastbourne Blue Ribbon Gospel Temperance Union, the Eastbourne Nonconformist Temperance Union, the Eastbourne branch of the Church of England Temperance Society, the Total Abstinence Society and many more linked with particular local churches. Not that temperance was solely a Christian matter. There were the Temperance Electors, the Eastbourne Temperance Council, the Eastbourne Temperance Building Society and, most gloriously, the events organised by the Eastbourne branch of the Temperance Cycle Club.

14 Hare (1988), *The Skeleton Army and the Bonfire Boys, Worthing, 1884,* Folklore, vol. 99.

15 Some bonfire societies were associated with a community or neighbourhood such as the Central Ward Bonfire Boys Society while others were connected with a particular trade such as in the Eastbourne Butchers' Amalgamated Bonfire Society.

16 Guy (1964), *Marching with Music,* Eastbourne Citadel Corps, p. 7.

17 *Ibid.*

18 *Worcester Journal,* 27 September 1884.

19 *Eastbourne Gazette,* 18 December 1895.

20 William Morrison was President of the Eastbourne Lifeboat Association, the Eastbourne Cricket and Football Clubs and heavily involved with the Rowing Club, Bicycle Club, Quoiting Association, Eastbourne Ornithological Society, Allotment Society and the Eastbourne Flower Show.

21 *Eastbourne Gazette,* 7 October 1891.

22 Briggs, *The Salvation Army in Sussex, 1883 – 1892,* in Kitch (ed.), (1981), *Studies in Sussex Church History,* Leopard's Head Press, p. 205.

CHAPTER FOUR

BLOOD ON THE STREETS

In its early years the Salvation Army experienced a remarkable growth in membership rapidly spreading from
established London roots to many other parts of the country.
Very soon the Army arrived in Sussex where it first became
particularly active in the far east of the county. Catherine
Booth had spent some time in Hastings in 1869 where her
preaching had been well received. The following year the
Hastings Station of the Christian Mission was opened in the
town. This was followed by further Missions in nearby St
Leonards, Rye, Ninfield and Boreham and further afield in
Brighton and Worthing.

As the Salvation Army grew so, too, did opposition against
it. By the end of the 1870s there were frequent newspaper
reports of violent attacks on Salvationists in many towns and
cities. At first most of these assaults were perpetrated by individuals and often associated with drunkenness. In time this
changed so that increasingly attacks were made by organised
groups. The first report of such was from Coventry in 1879
and there soon followed similar incidents in Whitechapel,
London and Basingstoke. A spate of attacks then took place
across locations in the south west including at Exeter,
Weston-super-Mare, Stroud, Salisbury, Honiton and
Torquay. The mission work of the Salvation Army and the
physical assaults which they suffered soon became of national
interest.

The disturbances then began to be felt in Sussex when violence broke out in Worthing in 1884. Angry and destructive mobs of several thousand roamed the streets attacking Salvationists and vandalising their property. When a crowd besieged the police station, some forty of the 4th (Royal Irish) Dragoon Guards were called from Brighton and the Riot Act had to be read before any semblance of order could be restored. Sadly for the Salvation Army the riots resumed in Worthing some little time later.

Salvationists in other Sussex towns also now came under attack. In nearby Brighton, a mob besieged the Citadel and attacked members as they attempted to process in the streets. Most dreadfully, in Hastings in 1883, Captain Susannah Beatty, who was one of the earliest converts to the Army, was knocked to the ground by rocks thrown at her and then kicked so hard in the stomach where she lay that her death some few years later was undoubtedly hastened by the injuries received on that day.

With violence going on both to the East and to the West it was not long before Eastbourne was drawn into events. Although there was only a small Salvationist presence of around twenty members in the town at this time it is clear that it was already being resented. On the evening of Good Friday 1883, as a service was being held in Longstone Hall, which was often used by the Army at this point, a crowd marched to the site accompanied by raucous music on tin pans and the like in mocking parody of their processions. Later over the Easter Bank Holiday weekend there were several well attended services held in the Hall. Preparations were being made for a planned visit to the town by the Salvation Army. At the Sunday evening service so many were present that some had to be turned away. The largely working-class congregation heard one of their number describe how he had been present at a local chapel that morning where the minister warned people to beware the Salvation Army and not to attend their meetings.

The next day there was a further service and a shared tea for two hundred people after which some marched the streets as a public witness to their faith and work. However, it did not go well for those in the procession who had heavy stones thrown at them. A few weeks later reports were made of further assaults on Salvationists.

On Sunday last, the members of the Salvation Army – the headquarters of which have been established at the Evangelization Society's Hall, Longstone-road, marched through some of the principal streets of the town. During the march they sang hymns in such a manner that they attracted the notice of some of the rough dwellers in the town, and the result was anything but creditable. On Monday the Salvationists held a service about mid-day, and about five o'clock a public tea was announced to take place, the admission to which was fixed at sixpence. It was further announced that at seven o'clock a service would be held in the Hall. Shortly before the commencement of the service a section of the Salvation Army returned from one of their marches and were just on the point of entering the Hall when some roughs, mostly boys, pelted them with gravel taken from a heap that had been laid down for use in front of a house on the opposite side of the way. The police were on the spot almost immediately, and quiet was soon restored.[1]

Later that night the Army held a service in the Hall which went on into the early hours, with admission by ticket only. Local residents complained of the noise from the Hall and stones were thrown, breaking two of the windows. The following week a letter appeared in the local newspaper from The Reverend Ernest Gill, Chaplain to the Salvation Army. He had been present and pointed out that the noise complained of was not, in fact, made by the worshippers inside the Hall but by the drunken mob gathered outside, some of whom later forced their way into the building.

It is no wonder, perhaps, that even at this early stage, concern should be expressed about the effect that these incidents might have on Eastbourne's tourism. It was felt that the town would develop a reputation for rowdyism which would keep visitors away.

There were other incidents at this time in which Salvationists were attacked individually and, seemingly, at random. In the summer, a man named Alfred Barrett was found guilty of assaulting Edward Dyer, a Salvationist. At the trial Barrett said:

"I am guilty of blacking his eyes, but not of assaulting him."
It would seem that the complainant is a member of the Salvation
Army and on Sunday [the] 29th he was marching with the rest
of the army, when defendant came up to him with blacking in
his hands which he blacked his eye with. Barrett said that when
he used the blacking Dyer said "Hallelujah, black it again."
Dyer said he did not remember using these words.[2]

Another incident occurred that same week. John Hickmore plead guilty to an assault on John Coleman outside Longstone Hall. At the time the complainant had been a member of the Salvation Army and, while he was marching, Hickmore had simply come up and punched him. The bench imposed no fine on Hickmore.

As 1884 began an editorial in the local newspaper struck a note which was more pragmatic.

The Salvation Army are not in good odour in the town; they
are looked upon as fair sport by the rude and ignorant and get
little sympathy from even the better educated, although all are
willing to allow that they strenuously work for the good of their
neighbours. They probably owe this ill-feeling, to a great
extent, to the noisy manner in which they go about their work
shouting and bawling, and playing on noisy instruments in the
streets, which cause great annoyance to the more peacefully

disposed and are repugnant to ordinary notions of the quietude
and peace of Christianity . . . My advice is to let the
Salvationists alone; if any good is derived from the movement,
it will survive, but if it is only an effervescent flash and is
productive of no permanent benefit, it will soon die out. Paltry
persecutions are unbecoming the spirit of the age.[3]

Indeed, for the first few months of 1884 while the situation
nationally and regionally was worsening, with escalating levels
of violence against the Salvation Army, in Eastbourne, at least,
it remained reasonably, though not entirely, peaceful.
However, antipathy towards the Army had by no means gone
away. In July there were rumours causing concern to many
locally that the Salvation Army was moving to new premises
in a building formerly used as a theatre because Longstone
Hall was felt to be no longer suitable. Although the move did
not happen, its possibility was regarded as an advance by the
Army and cause for concern.

The following month the Council decided that it must take
action over the whole issue of the disruptions in the town and
determined that they should work collaboratively with
Hastings Council where similar incidents were going on. By
the end of August the Council's stance had moved on so that
they would now seek legal powers to deal with the problem.
Accordingly, as a barrister at law, one Councillor Chambers
was asked to prepare a draft for a new Local Act. His work
was well received and its value acknowledged. The Bill
included a wide range of matters such as creating a new
Corporation Stock, an overhaul of the sea defences, the
licensing of street hawkers and those vehicles used for public
passenger hire as well as street and sanitation improvements
The situation regarding the ongoing disruption surrounding
the Salvation Army was to be dealt with simply as a matter of
a street traffic problem. The Council's view, however, was
that more power was needed to deal with the problems of the
Salvationists' processions.

All this time, at the height of the tourist season, the situation in the town was becoming an increasing cause for concern, especially in connection with the likelihood that local trade and business could suffer. This was reported by a local newspaper.

My attention has been called by several residents in Eastbourne to the great annoyance caused them on Sundays in consequence of the unseemly outdoor operations of the 'officers' and 'corp' of the Salvation Army at Eastbourne . . . That Sunday morning, being determined to ascertain the truth of the complaints which have been made to me, I took up a position near the drinking fountain, opposite the Leaf Hall. About half past ten the Salvationists arrived, formed a circle, and commenced their "manoeuvers". One young fellow, wearing a guernsey of deep scarlet, with various letters imprinted upon it, and having on his head a Salvationist cap, played the cornet and was evidently one of the "officials on the staff". Another individual had a larger brass instrument and when a hymn was sung, the two together succeeded in making a noise which excited the derision of many present. I could then well understand why those who lived in the neighbourhood made such bitter complaints in respect to these proceedings. There are many tradesmen residing in that neighbourhood who to my knowledge, work very hard during the week, and who look forward to Sunday as a day of rest . . . Surely we have enough churches and chapels in Eastbourne to comfortably accommodate all who desire to worship God without the introduction of this element of discord. I am told that at the evening gatherings, the scene is, as a rule, most discreditable, rough horseplay is freely indulged in and that the police have had to put in an appearance and restore order. It has been conveyed to me from several sources that unless some steps are taken by the authorities to prevent the nuisance, consequences of a discreditable character will in all probability be brought about.[4]

The issue came back to the Town Council the following week during a debate over the problems arising from coster-mongers obstructing the highway. Councillor Pearce took opportunity to raise the matter of what he saw as a similar obstruction caused by the Salvation Army when it met near to the fountain in Pevensey Road. He observed that it had become something of a nuisance and the police had no powers to do anything. Councillor Chambers assured Members that all this would be dealt with through the proposed new legislation he was preparing.

All this time trouble was brewing in the town. There were disturbances in Langney Road with rival processions of the Salvation and Skeleton Armies, the latter made up of gangs of rough young men. The disturbances went on for some hours.

> The Skeleton Army carried a huge white banner with a skull and other mocking designs thereon. Some hundreds of grown up men, youths, boys and girls formed in this procession. Comic songs, defiant expressions, and parodies of known hymns were used along several of the streets, and at one time when the two processions came into contact with each other a serious riot was feared. Many persons were rough handled and the police had much difficulty in preventing accidents and injuries. Several persons were knocked down during the collision and had to be rescued from peril by the police . . . Some of the Salvation Army members were much hustled about, the crowd present at this time being estimated at nearly two thousand persons.[5]

A few days later there were more disturbances when a large crowd formed outside Longstone Hall and made so much noise with singing and shouting that the worshippers inside had to stop the service. They were then pelted with rotten eggs and other offensive items on leaving the Hall. Later, Salvationists were jeered at and had so-called Chinese Lights thrown at them as they left the Hall.

Feelings in Eastbourne were clearly running high as a letter to a local newspaper makes clear.

. . . the inhabitants of Seaside, at any rate those in the imme-diate vicinity of the "fountain" (adjacent to the Hall) *are deeply grateful to the Skeletons for descending into the streets and clearing our main thoroughfare of the unmitigated nuisance, caused by the "Longstone Hall Mission" . . . These misguided people, to whom I give credit for good intentions assemble at the fountain several times a week and make night hideous with their boisterous style of worship, which has no other result than to bring religion into contempt.* The letter continued . . . *they have added tambourines and the blowing of horns to show their contempt for the comfort and quiet of their neighbours . . . which provokes . . . cursing mockery, and in many instances to a breach of the peace . . . The road leading from Pevensey road to Seaside road has many times been completely blocked for upwards of an hour at a time, without interference from the police; the mission have been quietly asked to desist during the dying illness of an old and respected inhabitant of Seaside but have shown their intolerance by not complying with this reason-able request. Is it any wonder, then, that force is opposed by force? The "Salvationists", to judge by numbers, are not a great success in Eastbourne, for they do not certainly exceed the numbers with which they started about two years since, viz., about twenty. The noise they create is out of all proportion to their strength. If anybody is to have pressure brought to bear upon them, it ought to be the "Salvationists" as they were the originators of the disturbance, and if they discontinue their orgies, the "Skeletons" will cease to trouble.*[6]

A rumour now went round the town that there was to be a major confrontation between the Salvation Army and the Skeletons, with the latter receiving extra help with confeder-ates from Worthing and Brighton coming to their assistance but this did not happen.

Within the week the whole matter came up again at a meeting of the Town Council. Councillor Keay moved that the Salvation Army be asked to stop their marching in the town. He also proposed that the police should be asked to deal with the Skeleton Army. At this, Alderman Morrison, later to be Mayor, suggested that his colleague might withdraw his second motion on the grounds that

> . . . if the first motion is successful there will be no necessity for the Superintendent of Police to take any action in respect of the Skeleton Army. (Most outrageously he went on to add), I have the very greatest sympathy with the Skeleton Army and have serious intentions of joining it myself (laughter), As regards the Salvation Army he did not think anyone could say good of it.[7]

The response of those at the meeting where this was said was to laugh at this suggestion, and it may have been said as a joke. However, in the context of the continuing threat of street violence against fellow citizens going about their business it does seem an injudicious remark to make by one who had been elected to serve as an Alderman. This does not seem to have been lost on Councillor Wenham when he observed, some years later, that

> To a man the mob believes rightly or wrongly, that the magistrates and the Mayor are in their favour . . . [8]

The Salvation Army now chose not to march out for three consecutive Sundays but, when they did, were met with confrontation. The Eastbourne Skeleton Army, which, on this occasion, included gangs of boys and youths, gathered threateningly outside Longstone Hall where Salvationists were at worship. So terrified were they that it was decided not to leave the Hall until all was clear and their safety secured.

The Council met again at the beginning of October and decided to make use of the Towns Improvement Clauses Act (1847) to deal with the problem. It was agreed that a legal team be appointed to work with Councillor Chambers on the draft Bill and, also, a Parliamentary Agent to promote the Bill once submitted. The contents of the draft Bill were to be published in the local press so that they might be broadcast widely. The Town Clerk was instructed to approach other Sussex coastal authorities at Brighton, Hastings, Shoreham and Worthing, where there also had been anti-Salvationist disturbances, inviting them to work with Eastbourne in a common course of action.

A meeting took place on the 17th of November in the Saloon of the Royal Pavilion, Brighton with representatives attending from Brighton, Eastbourne, Hastings, Worthing, Lewes and Shoreham. The purpose of coming together was to consider if any steps might be taken to regulate the processions of the Salvation Army. Following what was described as an interesting discussion those present agreed it was better for councils to deal with the matter individually rather than collectively.

Back in Eastbourne the matter of the anti-Salvationist disturbances was now a topic of interest at a newly established local debating society which enjoyed the name of the 'East-Bourne House of Commons'.[9] In mid-November they debated the so-called 'Street Procession Bill' which, sought to prohibit both the Salvation and Skeleton Army from holding public processions. The views put forward are rather revealing about the state of thinking in the town. At no point was the violence being meted out to Salvationists condemned. Some felt that the two rival factions were equally to blame while a number made criticisms about the Salvation Army, such as the inconvenience they caused to residents as a result of the riots and also that their musical bands were dreadful. There were only a few whose contributions could, in any way, be regarded as sympathetic.

Another disturbance now broke out in Eastbourne, reportedly much to the annoyance of a large number of local residents. A Salvation Army procession was confronted by a much larger group of Skeletons who hurled abuse at them along nearly the whole of their route before gathering outside Longstone Hall where they continued to shout as worship went on.

The unlikely coming together of different interests to combine against the Salvation Army locally was evident when the Bonfire Boys were involved in the celebrations for the re-election of Alderman G.A. Wallis as Mayor. Two large street processions went out, each with several hundred cheering marchers in fancy dress and both accompanied by bands. One of the processions even had the town fire engine at its head. When the marchers arrived at the Pavilion where the Mayoral Banquet was being held, two dozen of their representatives were invited to enter and march around the banqueting room to the evident entertainment and pleasure of the party. The Mayor was congratulated on his success and he then thanked the Bonfire Boys for their support. Afterwards the two processions formed up into one column which marched off, reportedly a mile in length.

It would seem clear from this incident that the Bonfire Boys were very popular in Eastbourne at this time and that this support may well also have extended to the Skeleton Army with whom they shared mutual association and many members.

There was now more violence when an Army procession from Longstone Hall was met by a group of some fifty Skeletons at the corner of Susan's Road where quite a scene took place. One of the leaders of the procession bravely shouted that 'the Lord would protect them' and began singing at which he was severely pushed, while several others were roughly handled. It was felt that only the presence of the police prevented the Skeletons inflicting worse violence on the marchers. Notwithstanding, the crowd followed the procession back to the Hall where it remained for some time shouting at the worshippers inside.

In early December a 'Great Meeting of Burgesses' was held in the Pavilion, Devonshire Park, to discuss the proposed Eastbourne Improvement Bill which aimed to deal with many issues of concern in the town. The packed audience was limited to property owners and ratepayers with Mayor Wallis and most of the Council also present. The meeting was much concerned with how the costs incurred by the proposed Bill were to be properly funded. The Council had only been incorporated for a year and, already, £40,000 was committed towards building and equipping the new town hall. However, what is particularly significant about what went on at the meeting is not the expressions of understandable and reasonable concern for fiscal propriety but rather the allegations made of bad practice on the part of some Council members. Such allegations, of course, may well be regarded as part and parcel of the badinage of local politics but, here, they were revealing of something possibly far more serious. Allegations against the Council were to be made on other occasions as well. Reuben Climpson, who had organised some earlier meetings opposing the Bill, claimed that he had only received the necessary papers for the meeting at 1 00 p.m. on that day but had, nevertheless, noticed some of the clauses which were in the earlier draft of the Bill had now been omitted. Climpson went on to suggest that, in any case, it could easily be argued that the Bill was not at all necessary as the Council already had access to a range of statutory powers which were, in themselves, sufficient to carry out the work planned in the Bill. What, then, was the point of the Bill? He proposed that the Bill was not required as there were sufficient existing powers open to the Council. Climpson explained to those assembled that at the meeting on the 30th of October the Council had voted 21:3 in favour of the Bill but when he had asked Members as to their votes nothing like twenty-one knew or could account for what they had voted on that occasion.

Alderman Morrison was now prompted to speak. He regretted that the papers had been received late and remarked

As to throwing dust in to the eyes of ratepayers he was sure none of the members of the council had ever such the slightest idea of doing any such thing . . . If they did as he hoped they would give the council authority to proceed with the Bill in Parliament, every question would be debated, every question would be voted upon, and they might rest assured that their interests were left in good hands.[10]

Climpson's proposal was then heavily defeated in a vote and the meeting soon came to an end in confusion and uproar.

What was the truth in this matter? Was it a matter of bad practice on the part of the Council, or their incompetence, or even false accusation by Climpson? The allegations would not go away. As later circumstances will make quite clear, the Council would be prepared, when necessary, to go to extraordinary lengths and take highly questionable means in order to secure the Improvement Act.

Amid continuing disturbances in the town a further meeting of the Council was called later in December to go through the contents of the Bill. There was a large attendance as members of the public were also permitted to be present. It soon became clear that matters were again not as they should be. Members had only received the papers for the meeting on that morning. Moreover, on examination of these papers it emerged that there had been changes to the draft Bill that had not been sanctioned by the full Council and of which members were ignorant. It was pointed out that since October there had been no meeting of the Council at which the draft Bill had been an item on the agenda. Even those councillors who sat on the Law and Parliamentary Committee had no knowledge of the changes. Incredibly, Councillors were being asked to vote, there and then, for their acceptance of a Bill containing four hundred and sixty four clauses and which they had not had opportunity to make adequate scrutiny. It was agreed to delay sending the Bill to Parliament until such time it could be properly examined and discussed. An adjourned meeting was held the following week. Following discussion, the majority on expenditure, it was put to the meeting that the Bill was in danger of missing the deadline for depositing at Parliament. Councillors were assured by the Mayor and Town Clerk that there would be opportunity to make amendments to the Bill even as it progressed through Parliament. On this understanding it was agreed to proceed and the Bill to be deposited.

Included within the Bill one particular clause was to become hugely important for the Salvation Army in Eastbourne. Clause 169 reads:

> *No procession shall take place on Sunday in any street or public place in the Borough, accompanied by music, fireworks, discharging of cannon, fire-arms, or other disturbing noise, provided that the foregoing prohibition shall not apply to any of Her Majesty's navy, military or volunteer forces.*[11]

Significantly, Clause 169 had neither been part of the earlier draft of the Bill nor, indeed, had it been included for publication in a local newspaper as part of the Council's public information and consultation process. Indeed, the only reference to it in the newspaper was paraphrased as

> *With respect to street traffic, we are seeking the usual municipal powers.*[12]

Furthermore, during the passage of the Bill through Parliament, Clause 169 was first struck out by Lord Redsdale, the Chairman of the Lords Committee scrutinising the Bill, only to be re-inserted later by a Commons Committee. When the Bill subsequently came to a vote in the Commons, Members did so without the full knowledge of the contents.

It was later pointed out in the Commons by Mr Fowler, M.P., that on this occasion Clause 169 had been

> . . . *inserted in the Bill by a majority of two in a Committee of four . . . this legislation was enacted behind the back of the House of Commons, that the House knew nothing of what was going on, the Committee did not say a word about the deviation from the law in the clause they inserted . . . was passed in this perfunctory manner and referred to in a general paragraph about clauses dealing with pleasure traffic boating and bathing . . .* [13]

That something had not been correct in the procedure was confirmed by Sir John Kennaway, M.P.

> *This clause was passed against the recommendation of the Home Office, and therefore, I think it fair to say the clause was passed behind the back of the House of Commons.* [14]

That there had, indeed, been a failure of due diligence in the parliamentary process was admitted by Arthur Arnold, M.P., who had sat on the Police and Sanitary Committee which re-inserted Clause 169 and had voted against doing so. The M.P. was moved to make clear his own regrets in the matter.

> *I think the power now exercised would not have been sanctioned had I carried my objection from the Committee to the House of Commons. I blame myself for having failed to call the attention of the House to the exceptional provision which the majority of the Committee had admitted to the bill . . .* [15]

It is, perhaps, no wonder that Bramwell Booth passed this comment on the manner of the parliamentary process involving Clause 169

> . . . *the members, not knowing that this particular clause which*

was aimed at the Salvation Army was in it at all . . . It was got by a trick.[16]

What was behind such an astonishing failure of parliamentary process? Why did members choose to demonstrate such blatant disregard for established procedure? Had members of the Council brought influence to bear? What may be made of it? After all this was not the first occasion when the Bill was associated with procedural irregularity.

Whatever the reason, the outcome was that the Bill passed into law. On the 6th of August 1885 the Eastbourne Improvement Act received the Royal Assent. It was now punishable by law to march through the streets of Eastbourne, while accompanied by music, on a Sunday. At one level it is simple enough to regard this as just an example of late Victorian English eccentricity but, at another, and in historical context, the use and enforcement of Clause 169 must be seen as an attack on personal freedom and religious liberty. Eastbourne Council had gained the power to prohibit what the Salvation Army would insist was an essential part of their street evangelism to the poor. The law may be upheld, or, indeed, broken but for Salvationists nothing was more fundamentally important than spreading the Gospel; neither the force of the law nor the rage of the mob would prevent them from doing so.

The next five years in Eastbourne were marked by a comparative calm. There were still letters to local newspapers complaining of the nuisance the Army caused, while from their pulpits clergy were still disparaging Salvationist methods. On occasion the Army did make attempts to march with music and the police were encouraged to deal with them accordingly.

In 1889 the Salvation Army renewed a long-standing interest in Eastbourne and made preparations to develop their mission work in the town. Catherine Booth was especially keen to see this happen. A series of articles in the *War Cry* laid the grounds. In September the magazine reported her saying that Eastbourne has been waiting for us a long time. On the 6th of September Field Commissioner Eva Booth, daughter of William and Catherine, steamed across the bay from Hastings to Eastbourne in an act of great theatricality.

The Salvation Army then turned attention towards a plan for new premises of their own. Until now they had worshipped in loaned or rented accommodation such as Longstone Hall, the New Temperance Hall and, on occasion, the Town Hall. The building of a new Citadel in Langney Road was announced in early September during a further visit to the town by Eva Booth. It was to be part of a national programme of expansion by the Army. The cost of the land and the building would be £2,000 of which the local Corps and their supporters would raise about one third. Tenders for the building work were invited in October. The Citadel was opened on the 9th of January 1890.

In the summer, the Army met with a significant degree of opposition to their work from the Council. Permission had been sought to hold short open air services, but only away from the main thoroughfare of traffic, and also that services might be held on the beach. The Army further requested increased police protection. At their meeting in early June the Council refused permission for the use of the streets, taking the view that under the law they could grant none the right to use a public place for that purpose. The Salvation Army, it was claimed, were under the same regulation as any other persons in this matter. The use of the beach was also declined. It was suggested that the Army approach the Chief Constable, Major Luxford, for his views on the matter of police protection. When the Chief Constable suggested this was not really his decision he received a considerable degree of opprobrium from both the people of Eastbourne and their councillors for his apparent lack of desire to be involved.

The meeting also heard how, in any case, the Salvation Army still presented a nuisance in the town. Councillor

Wenham reported complaints he had received from tradesmen in the east of the borough. He said that when recently the Army had held an open service they halted near to the business premises of the tradesmen while one of their number banged a big drum for some twenty minutes causing serious interruption all around. Newly elected Mayor Morrison then spoke, making his feelings about such incidents quite clear.

> *Personally it has been one of the most abominable nuisances to me for two successive Sundays. I speak feelingly, because anything approaching to blasphemy or irreverence are things I cannot put up with. I am not a good man at all, not a religious man . . . but I draw the line at that.*[17]

That the language Mayor Morrison used here was something less than judicious or appropriate to his office is clear. It would seem there was a culture and acceptance of such remarks on the Council. At the same meeting Councillor Tomkinson complained of noise outside All Souls Church when he and his family were at worship. He was unsure whether the noise was made by the Church Army or Salvation Army but felt moved to say if they persisted in coming he would put the hose on them, a sentiment for which he received the approbation of his fellow councillors.[18]

The Salvation Army did, however, receive some morale boosting news in the form of support from the Lord Chief Justice when he declared their right to play music while marching through the streets. He took the view that if the Army did not set out with the purpose of annoying people then it was acceptable and the sort of thing that in a free country those who were against it must submit. The Eastbourne Corps was now in quite a different strategic position. Their services were very well attended and local distribution of the *War Cry* magazine was rising to 1,000 security and despite growing opposition they could now advance with street evangelism. All this was just as well for a local newspaper had recently reported:

> *By a two thirds majority the Town Council of Eastbourne has declared war against the army and authorised the prosecution of its local leaders for perambulating the streets on Sundays with a brass band.*[19]

It was at this time that Mayor Morrison exhibited his antipathy towards the Salvation Army even in his private life, as the following report shows:

> *It seems that the fashionable congregation of St Saviour's Church is greatly disturbed in its devotions when the Army passed the edifice singing "Onward Christian Soldiers!" The Mayor who has taken the initiative on the Town Council, was so shocked the other Sunday that he actually rose from his seat in the midst of the service (the service had not commenced) and proceeding to the door, threatened the Army with the vengeance of the law if the band did not at once cease playing.*[20]

The prosecution of Captain Emily Goss and Sergeant-Major Hoadley now took place at Eastbourne Police Court where she was charged with having unlawfully sung in Tideswell Road contrary to the Eastbourne Improvement Act. The courtroom, which included Mayor Morrison and other members of the Town Council present, heard from a witness that the noise made by the Salvationists was detrimental to his lodging house business. The Bench dismissed the case but a pattern was emerging.

Another trial of a Salvationist went on some few weeks later when Bandmaster Appleby was charged with breaking Clause 169, having been in charge of a band of thirty to forty people on a Sunday. The case was brought by the Town Council. The courtroom was well filled and, again, included

Mayor Morrison and members of the Council. Mr Hall (Prosecution) put it that the Council had no feeling in the matter and that their only concern was for the law to be upheld. If the Bandmaster would consent not to do so again then the summons would be withdrawn. At this, Mr Colam (Defence) argued that this course was impossible for Mr Appleby and that, as a mere servant of the Salvation Army, he could give no such understanding. He went on to question the authority of the Bench to hear the case but, not surprisingly, they disagreed. Mr Hall reiterated his point about the attitude of the Council towards the Salvation Army:

> *I desire to disclaim on the part of the authorities here any feeling of any kind against the Salvation Army as constituted . . . But I wish to put it before you and I wish it to go forth to the public on behalf of the authorities here that the Salvation Army are not superior to any Act of Parliament; that like any mortals in this country, they are bound to obey the provisions of Acts of Parliament . . . No doubt the town of Eastbourne of the present time is a very flourishing place, and no doubt it is patronised by a large class of people of a very high position in life . . . These people, like absolute quiet upon a Sunday and have been brought up in the idea that absolute quiet on a Sunday is one of the privileges of the English.*[21]

The Bench unanimously found the case against Bandmaster Appleby distinctively proven and he was fined £2, with 13 shillings costs. After Mr Appleby and his fellow Salvationists left the courtroom they were heard singing outside.

In late April 1891 Herbert Booth, son of William and Catherine, and Commandant in charge of all Army operations in the U.K., wrote to Eastbourne Council. He enquired whether there were areas of the town which might be particularly badly affected as regards business and tourism were the Army to march through with music on a Sunday. He wrote:

It occurs to us that there may be certain portions of Eastbourne especially patronised by visitors, through which our marching with music on Sundays might be deemed by the authorities as injurious to the interests of the town. If this is so, and you will notify us of the same, we will carefully consider how far the success or the principles of our work will be sacrificed in in leaving these parts undisturbed by our music on Sundays. In the meantime I have instructed our Divisional Officer at Brighton to suspend any playing of our band on Sundays until I have received your reply to this letter . . . [22]

At the next Council Meeting a report was given on the matter by the Mayor, a member of the Watch Committee which had considered the application. Mayor Morrison said that the Watch Committee had no powers to limit the operations of Clause 169 and they bore in mind the many letters of complaint received prompted by the Army's practice of congregating in the streets. In what may be seen as something of a challenging manner he asserted that the Watch Committee, however, did have authority to take any steps that may be necessary were there to be a breach of Clause 169. Councillor Chambers was in full agreement, adding that if the Salvation Army did not like the Act then they should seek its repeal through Parliament. He also commented that as Eastbourne now had control over its own police force, the duty to enforce the law was to be even more keenly felt. He suggested that it was really a matter of maintaining the peace and quiet of Sundays for those who made weekend visits to the town. He concluded:

. . . that by persuasion and, if necessary, the strong arm of the law, we shall be able to control and to prevent these people making this mischief. [23]

In a remarkably well observed comment, tinged, perhaps, with something of a waspish sense of humour, Councillor

Wenham wished to draw attention to how matters were now developing in Worthing, a scene of dreadful anti–Salvationist riots only some seven years earlier. He pointed out that in a recent celebration in that town there had been a grand procession in which Mayor Morrison had accepted an invitation to walk at the head. The procession was led by none other than the same Salvation Army brass band which had played illegally in Eastbourne only a few weeks ago. Councillor Wenham encouraged the Council to adopt a similarly conciliatory attitude as their counterparts in Worthing had done. After considerable further discussion the Council voted to endorse the recommendations of the Watch Committee. Several members of the Salvation Army were present as observers to the meeting.

The Salvation Army now determined that they would make their stand for the right to march with music beginning on Whit Sunday, 17 May 1891. It was an appropriate day to choose. The custom of so–called Whit Walks in which a public profession of Christian faith is demonstrated was long established and very popular in late Victorian Britain.

It was to be a momentous day both for the Army and Eastbourne as this report makes clear.

Whit-Sunday will long be remembered in Eastbourne as marking the commencement of the struggle between the Salvation Army and the authorities respecting Sunday musical processions. It seems that immediately the Town Council had come to the decision by seventeen votes to five, to carry out the Act of Parliament in its entirety, the Salvation Army commenced active preparations for the fight.[24]

Just after 10 o'clock on that morning the Salvation Army brass band assembled in the Citadel and then marched out with the 'Blood and Fire' banner at their head. They were joined by other Salvationists, mainly women, and an open air service was held. A crowd of about two thousand gathered to watch what would happen. At the end of the service the Army members formed up into a procession and, at the command of the conductor, Captain Bob Bell, the band began to play. At this the police began to break up the procession and the crowd shouted loudly, pressing forward onto the marchers. Order was restored and a brief conversation between Captain Bell and Chief Constable Fraser ensued in which each man explained to the other their duties in the situation, the one to march, the other to arrest those who did so.

Chief Constable Fraser then fell back and the procession moved off with the band striking up as they went. A mob harried the marchers all the way back to the Citadel where showers of stones were thrown at the Salvationists. Captain Rebecca Chatterton spoke at a service inside in which she told the congregation that they meant to have the victory. The worship ended with Salvationists praying for the band, the Chief Constable and the town authorities.

There was another march out through the surrounding streets in the afternoon. Once more, a large crowd was attracted, many of whom by now were drunk. As hymns began to be sung accompanied by the brass band the crowd rushed forward brandishing bottles of beer and stout at the Salvationists.

Later that evening the Army held a third open air service, this time in Devonshire Place. As they marched away a huge, boisterous crowd followed them. Many local residents hung from their windows to gain a better view of the spectacle. Arriving at Bourne Street the mob made a sudden and determined rush at the marchers.

The scene of the wildest confusion followed, and the uproar caused was most disgraceful. Soldiers and lasses was shoved about and hustled, and it was only by the adoption of severe and summary measures that the police were enabled to quiet the row and enable the procession to continue its march . . . Considerable uproar also took place outside the army barracks,

*and the police experienced considerable difficulty this time in
dispersing the crowd, who lingered about, evidently loth to leave
a spot opening out, with the dark shades of night, such glorious
visions of a spree.*[25]

Inside the Citadel another service took place attended by
more than eight hundred worshippers. The Staff Captain
impressively urged everyone to pray for those who had
inflicted violence on them that day.

Bandsman Walter Guy

In his diary, Bandsman Walter Guy adds his eyewitness account of events that day, ending with something of a prophetic word.

The Eastbourne Band met for their first open-air meeting on Whit Sunday 1891 at the corner of Bourne Street and Ashford Road. A crowd of about 50–60 persons stood around and listened. When the Band marched away up Bourne Street – we had only gone about 30 yards – the Chief Constable stopped the march. There were a lot of boos and shouts and a demonstration against us, and the Chief Constable took the corps officer's name. He was summonsed to appear at the Police Court the next day and was fined £5 or a month in Lewes Prison. This was the start. Few if any of us thought of the almost unbelievable extent and at times almost tragic things that were to follow so small a beginning.[26]

What occurred on that Whit Sunday was hugely significant as it set the pattern of events that were to take place in the town each Sunday for more than a year. There would be many more episodes involving a much greater degree of violence.

In the aftermath of these events several members of the Salvation Army found themselves in court to answer charges of contravening the Eastbourne Improvement Act, and another of refusing to move on when requested from outside a sick person's home. They were found guilty and fined £5 each. No allowance was made for this being their first offence nor, indeed, that all Louisa Clark had done was to play her tambourine. One had furniture seized in lieu of payment while the rest elected to spend a month in Lewes Prison instead.

Walter Guy, again:

The first batch of prisoners, four in number and including Captain Bell and Sister Louise Clark, were taken to Lewes

BOROUGH
OF
EASTBOURNE
IN THE
COUNTY
OF
SUSSEX,

To *Louisa Clark*
of *43 Leicester Street, Eastbourne*
in the County of Sussex.

Whereas Information hath this day been laid before the undersigned, one of Her Majesty's Justices of the Peace in and for the said Borough of Eastbourne and County of Sussex, for that you on the *17th* day of *May* ------- 1891 at the Borough of Eastbourne in the said County, did *unlawfully take part in and form a member of a certain procession which took place on a Sunday to wit on the said 17th day of May in a certain street and public place to wit Bourne Street in the said Borough of Eastbourne the said procession be---* contrary to the form of the Statute in such case made and provided.

These are therefore to command you in Her Majesty's Name to be and appear on Monday, the *first* ------- day of *June* ------- 189*1* at Ten o'clock in the forenoon, at the Town Hall, being the Petty Sessional Court House in Eastbourne in the said County, before such Justices of the Peace for the said Borough of Eastbourne and County of Sussex as may then be there, to answer to the said information and to be further dealt with according to Law.

Given under my hand and seal this *26th* -------- day of *May* ------- in the year of our Lord One Thousand Eight Hundred and Ninety *One* at Eastbourne, in the County aforesaid.

Reginald Graham

Summons to the
Defendant upon an
information or com-
plaint.

[500—4.90.]

Louisa Clark Summons Sheet

Prison. They spent the time travelling in the train by singing. Upon arrival at Lewes they were marched by the police through the town to the prison followed by a crowd of about 100. At the entrance to the prison the Salvationists fell on their knees

in the roadway and prayer was offered by the officer in charge
of "Fort Rescue", Lewes, after which Captain Bell pronounced
the Benediction. Much handshaking and volleys of
"Hallelujahs" followed and in a few moments the doors closed
on the four 'offenders'.[27]

The matter eventually came to the attention of the House
of Commons when the Home Secretary was asked whether
the Salvationists might have their sentences remitted. This was
declined.

The week after Whit Sunday there was another march out
when a large crowd gathered and obstructed the path of the
procession. There was, again, violence of which some was
directed specifically towards Salvation Army women. One
woman was punched in the mouth and had the bonnet torn
from her while two others received such rough treatment that
they fainted. Attacks on Salvationist women would become a
major and characterising feature of the riots in Eastbourne.

The editorial in the *Eastbourne Gazette* at this time made
some important observations on two matters. First, it high-
lighted and was critical of the assaults on Salvation Army
women which were now emerging.

The Salvation Lasses were again somewhat roughly used by
the disturbing element, whose attacks on women must neces-
sarily be held up to public execration.[28]

Second, the editorial drew on some recent comments in a
Lewes newspaper which were very critical of Eastbourne
Council Members.

The seed of mischief was unquestionably sown on Sunday
week. The roughs then and since seem to have got an idea into
their heads that their own lawless acts are viewed by the author-
ities in only a semi-deprecatory light. This, unfortunately, is
only too true in regard to some members of the governing body

who have not been careful enough in preserving that requisite distinction between their private views and municipal life consistent with the dignity of the latter office.[29]

As a result of the recent disturbances eight more Salvationists were sent to Lewes Prison. In court with them was a Mr Smeeton, visiting from Finsbury, London who had walked behind a procession as a sign of his support. Unfortunately for Mr Smeeton, although he only walked a few yards, it coincided with the band beginning to play and so he was arrested for having broken Clause 169.

The disturbances continued on the next Sunday. When the Salvation Army marched out in the morning their procession included some reinforcements from the Hythe and Dover Corps. They were stopped by the police who took all thirty of their names. In the afternoon, a mob of several thousand attacked Salvationists who were at an open air service. The police sought to intervene in order to restore order but they, too, were attacked.

Walter Guy once more provides an eyewitness account of events:

One Sunday afternoon our open-air was at the top of Cambridge Terrace, Seaside. We were surrounded by a big mob who whistled, booed, howled and cursed horribly as we tried to sing and testify and pray. There were a good number of police there trying to look after us but suddenly each policeman got out his pocket book and pencil and took all our names and addresses. During the following week we all received a summons to appear at the police court, I shall never forget my Father who got hold of my summons, he came to me broken hearted and said "You have disgraced me Walter". He was afraid of the effect of my summons on his business which was with the gentry and tradesmen in the town. Poor Dad, I was sorry for him. We appeared in the court a few days later at 10 o'clock in the morning. The ordinary court was too small for such a number, so the Town Hall was made up into a court. We were put in two rows of chairs right across the hall and it was roped round and guarded by policemen. The court after the opening found that the cases took a lot of time and as 1 o'clock came it was adjourned for the lunch hour. To our surprise the police told us to go to dinner and come back at 2 o'clock and don't be late. I thought that was a very unusual thing to do. We arrived at 2 o'clock and the court resumed the hearing and later the magistrates adjourned to consider their verdict. We sat quietly waiting, there was a lot of going to and fro from the magistrates room and after a long consultation they filed back and took their places in court. The first question they asked was would we give an undertaking not to hold any more open-air meetings. Then they gave their verdict that all prisoners over the age of 21 years should receive the sentence of 1 month in Lewes Prison or pay the fine of £5. I was 19. The next Sunday we were all out as usual as though nothing had happened. We had lots of rough and tumble and crowds of people and the hall full of people and best of all many at the Penitent-form. To God be all the glory.[30]

A very revealing incident now took place in the Police Court when the Editor and Publisher of the *Eastbourne Standard* answered a summons of incitement to commit a breach of the peace. It was claimed that

. . on June 16th defendants did incite the public to commit a breach of the peace by lynching or in some other manner assaulting the Salvation Army by suggesting in their newspaper that if the police would leave the Salvation Army to the townspeople for a couple of days the Salvationists would have enough of it, and that the police were not justified in protecting the Salvation Army from assaults.[31]

When the case was heard the astonishing revelation declared by the prosecution was that, in fact, Mayor Morrison had a financial interest in the newspaper and owned the copyright to it. In his evidence the Mayor claimed he actually had nothing to do with the editorial direction of the *Eastbourne Standard* and only had a small financial interest in the newspaper of some £5 or £10. The Bench dismissed the charges on the grounds, incredibly, that that there had been no incitement to a breach of the peace. At the same court sessions three more members of the Salvation Army were sentenced to a month in prison for illegally marching with music! In late June, Field Commissioner Eva Booth made a four day visit to the town. So far she had been unable to take a more active role in events locally as she had been recovering from an accident. On Sunday morning the Field Commissioner led the Salvationists in their worship and also read to them a letter from her father, William, encouraging the Corps in their difficult mission work on the streets of Eastbourne. The letter, which was also published in a local newspaper told the congregation

> . . . *you have been driven into the present struggle by the enforcement of a clause in a Local Act of Parliament which is opposed to the general feeling of the people and the common law of the country, and which interferes with that work of evangelisation which we feel to be our sacred duty . . . You are therefore, I think, perfectly justified in asserting your rights, even though in thus doing you are opposed to the wishes of some of your fellow townsmen, and although it may entail upon you some amount of, not only inconvenience, but of actual suffering.*[32]

Field Commissioner Booth took opportunity during her stay in the town to visit Mayor Morrison at his home. After she had pleaded with him the cases of the increasing number of Salvationists who were being sent to prison, the couple knelt and prayed together. It was reported that the Field Commissioner was not favourably impressed with the Mayor's prayer, questioning its sincerity, seeing that it was he who had started and then continued with the prosecutions. The Field

Commissioner also visited Councillor Chambers who, it would appear from his comment, did not find the experience enjoyable: "*I had to submit to the assaults of Miss Eva Booth's tongue delivered in my own home.*"[33] During the month the numbers of Salvationists sent to Lewes Prison for breaking Clause 169 had grown considerably whereas those who assaulted them had not. Concern for this apparent disparity of justice was raised in the House of Commons by James Stuart, M.P., who asked the Home Secretary whether he was aware fifteen Salvationists, including three women, had been jailed for offences under Clause 169 but which were not offences under common law! He further pointed out how three men were convicted on the same day of assaulting Salvationists but had only been bound over to keep the peace and, given the inequality of these sentences, would he consider remitting the Salvationists' sentences? The Home Secretary replied that the alleged inequality arose from the application of different laws and found no ground for a remission of the sentences.In early July, at a meeting in the Town Hall, many ratepayers made complaints to the Mayor about the effects the disturbances were having on local business. Mayor Morrison got very agitated and, taking great exception to something he heard said by the minister of a local church who was sitting near to him, rose in great anger and waved his arm at the clergyman.

Further cases involving the Salvation Army now came to court. On Sunday the 12th a mob of some three to four hundred attacked a group of eight bandsmen. The next day, at the Police Court, James Moorton was accused of breaching the peace during the incident. He was from a family implacably opposed to the Army and who, himself, had been involved in a number of acts of disturbance. The Defendant was said to have shouted to the crowd "Come on lads" as he jumped in front of the procession. Fifty had followed him. A scuffle then broke out as the Salvationists attempted to defend themselves and their instruments. Four of them took hold of Moorton pushing him to the floor so that he might be restrained until the police could deal with the situation and for this he accused them of assault. A bandsman told the court how Moorton had threatened to punch him. At this Mayor Morrison, a Member of the Bench hearing the case, displayed a less than due judicial impartiality by laughing and going on to ask whether the police told the Salvationists that they were breaking the law in playing with instruments on a Sunday? The Magistrates found a breach of the peace had been committed but took the view this was partly caused by the Salvationists creating an excitement. Moorton was bound over with a charge of £20. The decision of the court gives a valuable insight to the low regard had for the safety and welfare of Salvation Army members at this time.

That same week James Gibbs appeared in court charged with assaulting Inspector Harry Plumb in the course of his duty, and also of a breach of the peace. Inspector Plumb told the court that he saw Gibbs deliberately rush at some bandsmen near to Leaf Hall. Together with Sergeant Ward he had apprehended Gibbs who then struck him several times and kicked out at him. Amazingly, the Bench dismissed the case as the Chairman said they had made allowances for the excited state of the police on the occasion. It is, perhaps, no small wonder that the opponents of the Salvation Army felt that not only the Mayor but also the Magistrates were on their side. A satirical verse which was popular at the time illustrated this feeling well.

Most noble Eastbourne Magistrates,
Whose judgements are sublime:
To beat a policeman is a joke,
But to beat a drum a crime.[34]

Despite this backdrop of continuing assaults on their Sunday musical processions the Salvation Army remained undeterred and began to make preparations to welcome back Captain Bell, Secretary Loadsman, Sergeant Baker and Sister

Louisa Clark from their term in Lewes Prison. They were
released on Friday the 10th of July and then spent a few days
of holiday in Brighton to recover from their ordeal.

On Thursday the 16th the newly released but now
refreshed Salvationists arrived at Eastbourne Railway Station
wearing prison uniform. Accompanied by Commandant
Herbert Booth they made their way into the station yard
where a gathering of around a thousand enthusiastic and
mostly uniformed Salvationists greeted them, the vast majority of whom travelled to the town on specially arranged
excursion trains. The crowded yard heard of their suffering
while in prison. Captain Bell had lost weight due to the
inadequate food and also developed sores on his shoulders
from sleeping on a plank bed. Others described how they
had to wear clothes full of mould and which was, at times,
verminous. They had even found maggots in their food.
Louisa Clark had also been detained in prison for a further
two hours after the others had been released as a punishment
for having pierced a page in a prison Prayer Book which read
'Blessed are they that are persecuted for righteousness' sake.'
Before Louisa finally appeared with the others, and thinking
she had not been released at all, her poor mother broke
down in tears and was only comforted by her daughter's later
arrival.

Commandant Booth now addressed the people. He
described Clause 169 of the Eastbourne Improvement Act as
'a smuggled affair' and wished strongly to condemn it

> . . . as being contrary to the general principles of English law
> and a violation of civil and religious liberty . . . we wish to
> express our strong disapproval of the action of the Town Council
> in refusing all our overtures of peace, and deliberately impris-
> oning members of the Salvation Army . . . We heartily welcome
> the four prisoners back to liberty and wish to express our deep
> sympathy with the seven prisoners now in Lewes Jail . . . leave
> us unmolested in the possession of the liberties which we have

inherited from our forefathers, and which are upheld by the
common law of England – to use the public streets for the procla-
mation of the Gospel.[35]

A big celebration then followed. Flags were distributed to
everyone and then forming up four abreast the procession was
led out with the banner of the Eastbourne Corps at the head.
The Household Troop Band followed together with the local
band. Field Commissioner Eva Booth and Staff Captain
Rebecca Chatterton rode in an open carriage and the former
prisoners in a 'War Chariot' over which hung a banner which
proclaimed 'Through Lewes Jail to Victory'. The procession
made a circular journey around the town before stopping at
St Aubyn's Road where a meeting was held. Commandant
Herbert Booth addressed the crowd. He called on the authorities in Eastbourne to stop their prosecutions of the
Salvationists and to administer the law impartially.

The celebrations continued on the beach throughout the
afternoon where Salvationists sang along to the music of brass
bands. Unfortunately, as the day wore on an unpleasant and
threatening atmosphere began to emerge. A man tried to drive
a horse and cart into the procession and was only prevented
from doing so through the vigilance of a nearby Police
Sergeant.

In the evening the Salvation Army held a service at the
Citadel and also a meeting at the Town Hall. At the latter,
Commandant Herbert Booth promised support for the
Eastbourne Corps and that some five thousand had already
volunteered, including five hundred 'dossers' or vagrants. He
predicted that the offending Clause 169 would be repealed.

After the meeting a terrible turn of events occurred. As
Salvationists made their way to the railway station they were
confronted by a hostile crowd of several thousand armed with
bricks, knives and pokers gathered in front of the station.
Several eyewitness accounts of what went on were published
locally.

The party who had met in the Citadel were the first to arrive.
Up to the Gildredge Hotel the band had continued playing and
there a rush was made at them. The Salvationists were
maltreated very roughly. efforts being made not only to strike
them, but to seize their caps and instruments. I saw about 12
fellows surrounding and severely ill treating a poor little fellow,
a Salvationist. It was most painful to hear the cries for help of
those who were thus beset. The Salvationist women, too, were
treated with very great brutality. Some of them were advised to
go into the station by the side entrance. They said "They were
not afraid" but they had not got far when they were attacked.
I assisted some to get into the station. I wish I had not been
there. I never saw a more painful or disgraceful scene. A ring
was formed and a man from Hastings and others spoke saying
"They must maintain their rights" and so forth. It was difficult
to hear what was being said. I believe they also sang the Bonfire
Hymn. When one of the Bands came up their white helmets
were pulled off and thrown up into the air in a shower.[36]

Another told:

I saw free fighting going on in all directions outside the station
and instruments flying about. One of the trombones was sent
flying over to the new bank, and people had to lower their heads
to avoid being struck with it. Every now and then the
Salvationists raised their hands and blew their whistles – I
suppose to indicate that they were safe. I saw several people
enter the station with blood trickling down their necks. Inspector
Houghton (a railway official) came in with a large number of
women and children and said "Push in there". Two or three
of the women were in a fainting condition, and the children were
crying and screaming. He had scarcely got the door closed when
a large body of the crowd followed the Salvationists through the
passages of the station hustling the bandsman. One or two
ladies belonging to Eastbourne were in the station and were so
frightened that they climbed through an open window into the
waiting room.[37]

A third was moved to say:

I have had considerable experience of riotous and disorderly crowds, but never have I seen anything to equal the scene outside Eastbourne railway station about 9 p.m. There had there such an assemblage of roughs as Eastbourne alone, I am sure, could never have provided. They were doubtless imported for the occasion and the local police were powerless to provide adequate protection to the Salvationists who were now flocking to the station on their way home. They were mercilessly assaulted on every hand, instruments broken and uniforms torn; women and men sharing in this rough treatment.[38]

Walter Guy was also present at the railway station that evening and he recorded his own account of what he saw being meted out to a young Salvation Army woman

One of our girls who was not successful getting in got caught up by some roughs who knocked her down and then taking her by shoulders and feet they threw her over the 6 ft. gate of the station. She was ill for a long time, but our women were full of courage and nothing could stop them.[39]

The Mayor and Watch Committee had become aware that the Army had something else now planned in Eastbourne and contacted the Home Secretary to ask whether it would be permissible, in the event of a riot, for the police to withdraw leaving the Salvationists at the mercy of the mob? The Home Secretary replied immediately and emphatically to deny this request. In response the Watch Committee sent a telegram to Scotland Yard asking for fifty Metropolitan Policemen to be sent on Sunday. This request was also denied so twenty extra policemen were drafted from other Sussex authorities to support the borough force.

Just three days after the violent scenes at the railway station a group of nine members of the Salvation Army Camberwell

Band arrived in Eastbourne. They could not know then but before the day was out the so-called Eastbourne Nine would be caught up in a quite singular incident. The bandsmen headed a procession from the Citadel towards the Wish Tower. The town was full of summer visitors who, together with locals, lined the streets to see the spectacle. The procession came to a halt at some waste ground between Tower Road and the sea. They formed a ring and an open air service began at which point some of the newly released prisoners spoke about their faith. When the Salvationists marched off the band began to play and immediately they fell victim to an attack. The police surrounded the marchers for their protection and marched alongside towards the Citadel. Arriving in Langney Road the procession was at once confronted by a mob of several thousand which included the Mayor who was cheered enthusiastically as he passed among the crowd. The atmosphere was tense and a riot seemed imminent. At one point someone in the crowd loudly shouted that the Mayor had instructed the police to 'lock them up'. Mayor Morrison would later deny ever having made such a pronouncement and the facts are, of course, always uncertain, but there is much evidence to question his denial.[40]

The nine bandsmen were arrested and marched through jeering crowds of such hostility towards them that the police constables had to protect them all the way back to the police station where a crowd had gathered to clap and cheer as they went inside.

Local public opinion was certainly on Mayor Morrison's side in this matter. A local newspaper reported:

> *At last the Mayor screwed his courage to the sticking place and ventured on arresting the bandsmen . . . The legality of the vigorous steps taken on Sunday may lead to long and expensive litigation . . . no reasonable man can deny that the Mayor is justified in taking any lawful means to enforce the Eastbourne Improvement Act, and, in the interests of the whole town, it is*

essential that the unhappy dispute now raging should be put to an end to at the earliest possible moment.[41]

The same edition of the newspaper also included a letter from Councillor Chambers in which he described the Salvation Army as being akin to French Communists, German and Russian Nihilists and universal Anarchists.

The day after their arrest the nine bandsmen appeared in the Police Court to answer charges of both acting in such a way that a breach of the peace would arise and also of forming part of an unlawful assembly. It is remarkable that having already been involved in their arrest, it was Mayor Morrison who now preferred the charges. He made his position clear from the outset in addressing the Court

> *The lives and property of the citizens of this town are, unfortunately for them, I would say, in my hands. The unfortunate scenes which took place yesterday were in my belief caused by most ill-judged language used by Mr H. Booth at the Town Hall on Thursday last (applause) . . . If Mr Herbert Booth is able to say he will send down people here, we can say for one Sunday at least we put a stop to this most infamous, degrading, and atrocious movement which has taken place (applause).*[42]

These words would eventually come back on Mayor Morrison.

Mr Clare (Defence) then addressed the Bench to make the point that the Mayor was both the Complainant and the Prosecutor in this case which was both unprecedented and unfair. The case was adjourned until Thursday the 23rd. The Mayor was cheered on leaving court.

Later that week the Court sentenced three more Salvationists to a month in Lewes Prison, followed two days after with a further five being jailed. These included a blind man and a woman of poor health who had sole support of her elderly mother and disabled daughter.

At the adjourned trial the nine bandsmen were charged with unlawful assembly but as matters were coming to a conclusion the prosecution added a second charge of conspiracy at the very last moment. The Bench decided to commit the men for trial at Lewes Assizes.

The Salvationists appeared at the Assizes on the 8th of August. Mr Justice Hawkins, who heard the case, began with an appeal for the two sides to reach a compromise settlement. He suggested the band did not play for two Sundays while the Council considered a proposal that any procession by the Salvation Army should be limited between their barracks and waste ground at the Crumbles. Within two days the Council had rejected the proposal and passed a resolution that they wished the Sunday band issue to be settled through the courts. Councillor Chambers was particularly strong in his rejection of the suggested compromise describing it as altogether inadmissible and indefensible. The Council was not altogether alone in taking this view as a petition, more than ten yards in length and containing over half the names on the East Ward Burgess Roll, was deposited at the Town Hall. The petition requested that the same degree of protection from the nuisance of the Salvationist processions should be afforded to all parts of the town. The Army's solicitor now successfully applied for the trial to go to the Central Criminal Court in London on the grounds that a fair trial would be unlikely if it were heard in Sussex. There was also the risk of considerable public disorder were the trial to go on locally.

Matters continued to develop in Eastbourne. At their meeting in early August the Council received a recommendation from the Lighting and General Purposes Committee that the Salvation Army should no longer be permitted to let the Town Hall on a Sunday all the time they continued their processions on that day. The Council duly agreed.

As a stream of prisoners now returned from Lewes they told of their experiences. A Salvationist called Hollamby, like many others, spoke about the poor food he had endured. On his first Sunday he had been given a piece of bread with a maggot half an inch long in it. At the same meeting Edith Maynard told the people she was prepared to go to prison for six months if it would get the Mayor saved.

A welcome outside Lewes Prison

All this time the Army kept marching and the rioting continued. Salvationist women were again a target for ferocious assault. At a trial in the Police Court a Sergeant gave evidence of an attack on two Salvationist women who had been knocked down in a riot. He was unable to identify their assailants as so many blows had been struck on the women.

At the end of that month a heated debate went on at a Watch Committee Meeting. Chief Constable Fraser put to Members that he felt under constraint in his efforts to suppress the rowdyism of the mob. Several Councillors spoke in support suggesting that the nominal penalties handed down by the magistrates acted to encourage the mob in its lawlessness. Mayor Morrison took umbrage at all this and hurriedly left the meeting threatening to resign.

In early September the Mayor took the decision to publish a proclamation in the town. It makes for extraordinary reading in terms of its intended suppression of both religious and civil liberties in Eastbourne. It was

> . . . a proclamation forbidding any procession with bands, and warning people that by forming part of a disorderly assembly they would subject themselves to punishment for any crimes committed by anyone during the disturbance. It was also notified that the police if ordered to clear the streets, would do so without respect of persons, and that any idle or disorderly individuals would be arrested.[43]

In taking this truly remarkable action the Mayor was actually subverting a whole raft of laws.

The Council also took opportunity at this time to reinforce the borough police by recruiting one hundred and twenty 'Specials' as members of the regular force were by now exhausted through their repeated extra Sunday duties. However, it cannot have been a simple naivety in the recruitment process that a considerable number of these men were, in fact, members of the Skeleton Army and widely known for their opposition to the Salvation Army. Indeed, one man had been found guilty of assault on a Salvationist in court on Friday only to be sworn in as a 'Special' by the Mayor on Sunday. Many of the new recruits were locally regarded as of dubious character. While the 'Specials' were held in reserve at the Town Hall they vandalised part of the building and spat over much of the floor. When it was discovered that one of their number had associations with the Salvation Army he was surrounded and tormented until he broke down in tears. Many got drunk having gone to the nearby New Inn Hotel where the landlord, himself, had been in court on charges of assault on a Salvationist and damage to his instrument.

In keeping with the spirit of Justice Hawkins' compromise suggestion, the Salvation Army marched out on Sunday but took no instruments with them. Nevertheless, the mob still attacked, focussing much of their ire on the women in the procession. Later, in the Police Court, Chief Constable Fraser was to tell the Bench that the Salvation Army had not carried their instruments for the past few weeks but continued to be attacked.

Although there was no major rioting during September it was now quite commonplace in Eastbourne for assaults on Salvationists to continue. The Police Court was kept busy with a steady flow of cases which told a litany of cuts and bruises, damage to uniform and instruments and vile verbal abuse thrown at men and women alike. The area around the Citadel was now a dangerous territory.

There were still many reports of violence against Salvationist women. Louisa Clark was knocked down and struck on the temple while on the ground. An eighteen year-old woman suffered a severe blow in the breast which was found to have caused some internal injury and another was kicked unconscious. The town magistrates continued to hand down lenient sentences on those found guilty of such crimes expressing the view that they could not forget the Salvationists were the 'aggressors' as, but for them, the disturbances would not go on. Some critical voices were raised so the Mayor took opportunity to write a letter to *The Times* in which he declared that

> . . . *the magistrates, and the Town Council have done, and are doing, and will continue to do, their duty in endeavouring*

to maintain law and order and to prevent disturbances of the
peace, and it is surely not too much to ask the Salvation Army
to refrain from breaking the law.[44]

Bramwell Booth was not slow to reply asking why it was
that the Mayor had nothing to say about

> *. . . the thieves and rowdies, the prize fighters and boozers*
> *who have been allowed to gather together Sunday after*
> *Sunday, primed with liquor for the attack on inoffensive men*
> *and women, who are known never to return a blow, and who*
> *may, therefore, be struck by any coward . . . It is admitted*
> *our people have suffered the spoiling of their goods, that their*
> *clothes have been torn off their backs in the open streets, and*
> *they have been mobbed, and hooted, and stoned, and carried*
> *away fainting from scenes that would have disgraced Magdala*
> *or Coomassie.*[45]

In early October Mayor Morrison was re-elected to serve
a third term in office and he was immediately embroiled in
controversy over the disturbances. Mr Sheward, a council
official, had written a letter to a Brighton newspaper in which
he accused the Eastbourne authorities of a signal failure to see
that justice was administered fairly. The letter told of the many
Salvationists who had been both brutally assaulted and sent to
prison for marching with music, while their assailants had
gone relatively unpunished. The Mayor would not permit the
letter to be read out at the meeting and went on to say that
the writer, as an employee of the Council, was deserving of
its censure. At the same meeting, Mayor Morrison referred to
a report in London newspapers and elsewhere which claimed
to be based on the proceedings of the last Watch Committee
Meeting at which, it was said, that he had given justification
for the active opposition of the Salvation Army seen so regularly in the town. He denied the comment and wished to
pursue a case for libel through the courts.

Meanwhile, assaults on Salvationists increased. During a procession in which all instruments were carried in bags but not played, the marchers were attacked with clubs and stones by an angry mob. One of the marchers was hit so hard on the head that he bled profusely and was left partly paralysed. His assailant was an off duty 'Special'. Afterwards the mob broke into the Citadel and lay ransack to it.

A major riot broke out a week later when a crowd of three thousand people attacked a procession immediately on the band starting to play. The banner was torn, instruments were smashed and Salvationists suffered many injuries. Later, a Councillor who was known to be sympathetic to the Salvation Army, was recognised by a gang outside the Citadel and had to seek police protection.

Battered Bugle

Threats of attacks were now made on the Citadel building. Barricades on the doors and windows were put in place and a wooden fence ringed the premises. It was as though a siege was in place; and indeed it was. A mob of two thousand more now waited outside to attack Salvationists returning from a march out and went on to smash about thirty of the building's windows. The Mayor was present at the incident.

Violence was again the order of the day soon after when a crowd of several thousand attacked a procession. The Standard Bearer was cruelly treated by being stood on his head and his face dashed against a tree. Women were again targeted. Three were thrown to the ground and jumped on by a group of men. When the Salvationists re-started their worship the mob broke out into song with "We'll hang old Booth on a sour apple tree". Mayor Morrison was again present and loudly cheered by the crowd.

Whenever the Salvation Army marched out from the Citadel they were attacked. So common did it become that crowds of residents and visitors, knowing the time of the procession, would gather in anticipation of the spectacle. Onlookers lined the streets to see marchers have flour, eggs and yellow ochre thrown at them in Terminus Road. This time the one thousand strong mob carried heavy sticks and clubs to bludgeon the heads of the marchers. Some women were violently thrown to the ground and trampled underfoot while one was beaten as she lay on the ground. A woman had her forehead laid open with a deep gash while another had her bonnet ripped from her head and arm cut. On seeing the results of their endeavours the mob clapped and cheered loudly. In what may be described as an act of some degree of sexualised misogyny the mob also deliberately seized and trampled the women's uniform dresses causing them to be drawn over their heads, exposing them. Sexual humiliation had now been added to the armoury brought to bear on the women of the Salvation Army.

When Mayor Morrison was re-elected just a few weeks before, the occasion prompted a letter to a local newspaper in which it was suggested that

[the] unhappy dispute with the Salvation Army has been a considerable anxiety and difficulty to his worship; but, by

strictly maintaining the Queen's peace in the town, he will have
a very fair prospect of winning the battle against the Boothite
party.[46]

The issue of violence on Salvationist women was raised in
a letter to a London newspaper in which the writer made an
appeal to Englishmen to go down to Eastbourne to protect
the lasses. So it was that Charles Mooney together with five
other like-minded men travelled to Eastbourne to offer
support and protection to the women of the Salvation Army.
Mooney was clearly no shrinking violet. Arriving in town he
mounted a palisade and addressed the crowd:

> . . . *I am not a Salvationist, I am I am not a religionist. I come*
> *here merely as a man, and I speak to you as Englishmen like*
> *myself. I come here without any idea of defending the Salvation*
> *Army or their band. I personally think that their band is a*
> *cursed nuisance (deafening cheers). But let me have a word*
> *. . . I have been in many places all over the world, but I have*
> *never seen in the widest places or the maddest diggings a woman*
> *beaten or trampled upon (interruption). That is why I have*
> *come to-day to make one appeal to you Eastbourne men – to*
> *you Eastbourne Englishmen . . . Will you promise not to touch*
> *a woman? For God Almighty's sake let the women alone.*
> *They are weak; they are helpless; they might have been your*
> *mothers or sisters . . . it is only a coward that can touch a*
> *woman.*[47]

Sadly, Mooney's words fell on deaf ears. In the same edition
of the newspaper a letter appeared from a local Salvationist
woman, Lucy Fenner. She had recently been caught up in a
riot during which she was violently thrown to the ground and
kicked where she lay. In another letter Charlotte Bradshaw,
also a local Salvationist, told how in the same riot she had been
repeatedly thrown to the ground and kicked causing a severe
injury to her arm. She had her bonnet ripped from her head

and heard someone say that they have it for Bonfire Night. Incredibly, the newspaper did not withhold details of the women's addresses.

These continuing incidents were of national interest and often taken up by the press from outside Eastbourne. Mayor Morrison was interviewed by the *Daily Graphic* during which he refuted newspaper reports about violence, going on to make a quite remarkable statement:

> *I have never seen a woman ill-treated. I have seen no man injured.*[48]

Chief Constable Fraser was interviewed at the same time and confirmed the Mayor's assertions as to exaggerated newspaper reports. He, too, made an exceptional and somewhat enigmatic comment:

> *I don't say women have not been knocked down, because, to my knowledge, they have . . . I have never seen a woman knocked down on Sundays.*[49]

In the same week Mayor Morrison was part of a crowd of between three and four thousand people gathered threateningly outside the Citadel. It was reported by a local newspaper of the Mayor that

> *. . . he was more excited than anyone there. Clearly he felt the load of his responsibility – felt it overmuch, one could not help thinking.*[50]

Local feeling on the issue of the disturbances may be measured in the popularity which the Mayor continued to enjoy locally. A presentation was made to him in appreciation of the way that he had personally dealt with these difficult matters to the honour and credit of the community. The position taken by the Mayor towards the Salvation Army was also endorsed at the elections in the East Ward in which both Districts returned candidates known for their opposition to Sunday musical processions. When Mayor Morrison appeared at the Result both he and the two winning candidates were roundly cheered.

In December the case involving the nine Camberwell bandsmen was heard in the Central Criminal Court. They each answered an indictment charging them with conspiring with other persons to contravene the provisions of the Eastbourne Improvement Act. There were several other counts in the indictment charging each with unlawful assembly. Mr Graham (Prosecution) told the court how the men had been observed by police arriving in the town and that later on Chief Constable Fraser had expressly instructed them they would be acting illegally were they to play their musical instruments; when they did so, arrest followed. Mr Willis (Defence) put to the jury that no action taken by these men had, in any way, violated the Eastbourne Improvement Act and went on to argue for religious liberty for all. In his summing up of the case, the Judge attributed no blame to the Mayor or the police authorities but felt that the crowds in Eastbourne had behaved disgracefully. He underlined the legal point that an Act of Parliament was the law and until it ceased to be so, all must obey its provisions, notwithstanding any circumstances. If there were those who objected to a particular law then they should seek to have it repealed. After a deliberation of only some twenty minutes the jury found each of the men guilty of unlawful assembly and not guilty of conspiracy. The Judge was not prepared to accept the guilty verdict and referred the case on to the High Court.

From the point of view of the Eastbourne authorities the outcome of the trial represented a strong measure of success. They had wanted an authoritative legal decision as to whether Clause 169 was part of a bad law and Justice Hawkins had been very clear: whatever objections there may be to Clause 169, it was the law. On his return from London, Mayor

Morrison was afforded a hearty welcome at Eastbourne railway station. He was met by a large and jubilant crowd who, taking the horses from his carriage and bearing torches, escorted him all the way to his home.

Perhaps it was the triumph of the moment which caused Mayor Morrison to act as he then did in issuing a second proclamation in Eastbourne. It went so far as to forbid

> . . . the holding of meetings, or delivery of addresses, in streets, parades or foreshores by any person or persons . . . on Sundays.[51]

The proclamation was first challenged locally not by Salvationists but by the Wesleyan Methodists who soon announced their opposition. The Salvation Army sought legal advice on the matter from Sir Charles Russell and were pleased to receive his view that, in fact, the proclamation was without legal foundation. Not surprisingly, the proclamation was quickly withdrawn.

The Salvation Army now introduced new tactics for their Sunday musical processions. Rather than meeting to form one marching column they would come together in smaller groups simultaneously in several different locations. This move made the task of policing a great deal more complicated. It also left the marchers at the mercy of the mob. It was decided, when attacked, they would simply submit to their assaults and take no steps whatsoever which would enable the police to bring their assailants to court. The move both made the point and presented problems to the authorities. Eastbourne's reputation became even more sullied. However, even those cases which did eventually come to court were largely futile. After the Citadel had had some thirty windows broken at the end of October, George Tobutt, a general dealer, came to court to answer a summons for their damage. The magistrates found Tobutt not guilty despite police evidence to the contrary.

An article, very revealing of attitudes in the town, appeared in a local newspaper at this time. It was simply a list of seven Salvationist women who had each suffered assault in recent weeks. The injuries received included paralysis of the arm due to having it twisted, being beaten with sticks and kicked unconscious, being knelt on the stomach so hard that food could not be retained and other awful life changing injuries. The article was just a list; there was no comment, critical or otherwise and was sandwiched between the Weather Report and an article urging local players to organise a cricket festival in the town.

Events were now about to move in a very different direction. In reply to a letter from a fellow M.P. who took the view that the Eastbourne Improvement Act had not worked, the Solicitor-General, Sir Edward Clarke, wrote indicating his support for the repealing of Clause 169. He said that the clause was

> *a serious and unjustifiable interference with a public right . . . I hope you will help repeal this exceptional law. The rights of public meeting and public processions are so important that I look with great jealousy on any attempt to limit or infringe them.*[52]

The Salvation Army responded and took new steps in their hard struggle for religious liberty. They would seek a change in the law by Parliament through the removal of Clause 169 from the Eastbourne Improvement Act.

The first few days of 1892 began with a series of unusually determined assaults on the Salvation Army even though, again, no instruments were played but only carried. Before marching out on Sunday the 3rd of January each individual member in a procession had confirmed to their officers that they were prepared to be imprisoned for their actions. To facilitate this further all had written down their names and addresses to be handed over to the Chief Constable when the case arose. As the procession left the Citadel an angry mob followed them all the way through the town to the beach adjacent to Grand Parade. Here the Salvationists formed a ring, linked arms and knelt to pray. Soon even more people gathered to join the mob and tension ran high. After a short while an attack turned the beach into a battlefield. So ferocious and determined were they that it was necessary to use mounted police to drive the mob back. As well as suffering considerable injuries the Salvationists also lost a good deal of their uniforms and instruments, many of which were hurled into the sea. In acts which again may be viewed as sexualised misogyny some of the women and young girls had their dresses ripped open. Eventually the Salvationists managed to gather on the promenade from where the police escorted them back to the Citadel. This incident rather showed that opposition to the Army's musical processions was but a subterfuge to suppress and persecute them; there had been no music throughout.

On the return march there was more disorder and, at one point, the procession was driven into by a man driving a pony and trap. A few days later the Watch Committee discussed the matter of these recent disturbances, especially in the light of what they regarded as inaccurate reporting in the press. It was agreed to send a copy of the Chief Constable's report to the newspapers concerned. The Watch Committee would truck no divergence from their own narrative of events.

By the end of the month the Court of Crown Cases Reserved set aside the earlier conviction for unlawful assembly which had been handed down to the nine Camberwell bandsmen. In his summing up Justice Hawkins said there was

not any evidence on which a reasonable jury could have acted in finding the defendants guilty of an unlawful assembly . . . no one had suggested that on that occasion anything was said or done by the Army or the band which in the least degree could have tended to provoke any human being that they intended a breach of the peace . . . It would be impossible to conceive of a more peaceable body of men.[53]

News that the verdict had been quashed was not well received by many back in Eastbourne and it prompted an even greater degree of hostility towards the Salvation Army. The Watch Committee decided to instruct the Chief Constable to make use of the entire borough police force to prevent any playing of musical instruments in processions. As matters were to develop it was rather fortunate that the police were present in strength. On the next Sunday a procession left the Citadel and a large and unfriendly crowd first surrounded and then accompanied the marchers as they made their way through the town before arriving just east of the Wish Tower where even greater numbers confronted them. A strong cordon of police had to be quickly placed around the marchers who, by now, had formed a ring for worship. As the band began to play the mob surged forward knocking many to the ground. In the ensuing turmoil the police fought with the crowd and finally saw them off allowing the procession to form up on the promenade. When the marchers arrived back at the Citadel they were assaulted again despite a sizeable police presence. It was only the good work of the police which prevented the mob from forcing their way into the building to wreak even more havoc.

At the beginning of February there were extraordinary scenes of mob violence in Eastbourne. Feelings were running high in the town and, it was said, the crowds were larger and more violent than any previous Sunday. The month saw the second anniversary of the opening of the Citadel and rumour had spread that several Army brass bands had been ordered to visit to be part of celebrations. When a procession left the Citadel on its way to the Wish Tower a large crowd walked alongside mockingly singing parodies of Salvationist hymns. Hundreds of onlookers at windows and balconies and some even in carriages drawn up close by were eager to see what would happen. The marchers managed to get onto the beach and, as Staff-Captain Rebecca Chatterton began the service, the mob rushed forward shouting that they would throw the worshippers into the sea, and made strenuous efforts to seize the banner. The diligence of the police denied the rioters their intention. Having failed to get at the Salvationists the mob now threw large beach stones at both them and the police for a sustained period of thirty minutes. When the service was finished the procession formed up and made its way back to the promenade where there was an attempt to seize the Army banner. As the marchers drew level with the Burlington Hotel the mob made a second and sustained attempt at taking the banner. Eventually, they were successful and the banner was torn to shreds. Attacks were now made on individual Salvationists. Many had their uniform torn from them and, once again, women were targeted for violent assault. When the procession reached the Citadel it had to force a way to the door through a hostile crowd. Staff-Captain Jackson, who had been beaten to the ground and kicked repeatedly earlier that day bravely declared that the Army had no intention of stopping their processions; the imperative to evangelise was paramount.

Prompted, perhaps, by the passage of the repeal Bill through Parliament, several well-known M.P.s visited Eastbourne to observe what was happening in the manner of a fact finding mission. The Parliamentarians bravely mingled with the crowds and must have been shocked by what they witnessed. The Duke of Portland also came to see the riots and, amazingly, the Prince and Princess of Wales and their family, who were staying at Compton Place, saw the scene where a riot had only until recently taken place.

Eastbourne Council now took the initiative. Mayor Morrison met with Admiral Field, the sitting M.P. for Eastbourne, to make plans on how best to oppose the Bill in Parliament. The Mayor also wrote to all other local councils in the South East seeking their support in the legal fight against repeal. The councils were specifically asked that, if they supported this position, they should contact their local M.P. putting the case that the Bill should be opposed in the Commons. The Council also agreed to hold a vote in the town on the matter of retaining Clause 169. The result was overwhelmingly in support of keeping the clause, with a majority of 7:1. Armed with this local poll of opinion the Council could now put the argument to Parliament that, for the sake of democracy, the clause must stay in place.

As the Council and the Salvation Army prepared for Parliament to consider the repeal Bill, the riots continued in a familiar pattern. As marchers left the Citadel they were immediately surrounded and harassed by a large crowd gathered outside. Such was the size of the crowd that even mounted police together with constables on foot struggled to maintain order. When the procession, which once more carried no musical instruments, arrived at the beach adjacent to Devonshire Place the police stopped them going any further. The crowd made a sudden surge on the marchers and there was uproar and chaos. Many Salvationists were knocked down and kicked. When the mob attempted to seize the banner, the bearer and several others were driven across the road onto the palings of the Cavendish Hotel. Many had uniform damaged and even Bibles were torn to pieces. Women were singled out for vile treatment once again having their clothes ripped and being beaten unconscious.

In a tactical move the Salvation Army played no music in their processions from November 1891 until March 1892. However, throughout this whole period the violence of the mob and the implacable opposition of the Council continued. Increasing numbers of Salvationist women reported assaults of a sexualised nature and many others spoke of how they had been throttled, kicked unconscious and trampled underfoot. During one procession at least twelve women were knocked down and beaten savagely. So extensive were Ruth Parson's injuries from kicks to the back and head, that she had to be dragged from the crowd unconscious and brought back to the Citadel. A doctor was called who decided that the still unconscious woman had to be taken to the Princess Alice Hospital. As Ruth was carried to a waiting cab the crowd gathered around her laughing and shouting that it was all a hoax. When the cab drove away they mockingly formed up on either side of the roadway and hissed as it passed them.

The persecution of Salvationist women even extended to their medical treatment. A young woman was admitted to hospital only to be hurried through her treatment that her injuries might be understated to the public. This same poor woman was then humiliated as the hospital authorities told it abroad that she and her clothes were filthy and both had to be washed while in their care. When the issue of these assaults on women came up at a Council meeting in early March the views expressed are rather telling. A Councillor argued that anyone found guilty of such assaults should be firmly dealt with by the law. However, another member suggested that the women actually did not mind the attentions of the mob, while some went so far as to say that, in fact, the women actually rather liked it!

During March the Eastbourne Improvement Act (1885) Amendment Bill made its way through Parliament. In the Commons, Henry Fowler, M.P. for Wolverhampton East, explained to the House how it had only been through highly questionable means that Clause 169 had become legislation. He went on to comment

> . . . on behalf of these poor Salvation Army people, persecuted as they have been, harried as they have been, sent to prison as they have been, that I ask the House of Commons to wipe from the Statute Book a section which has enabled religious persecution to be carried on to the disgrace and shame of the last decade of the Nineteenth Century.[54]

He was supported in this by Mr Courtney, M.P., who argued that really it was the Eastbourne magistrates who were responsible for disorder in the town.

> *They are the real lawbreakers; it is their conduct which has stim-ulated the mob to disgraceful violence. All the talk about preserving the quiet of Sunday for the benefit of Eastbourne invalids is moonshine. Mr Morrison and his colleagues had made up their minds to put the Salvation Army down. They objected, not so much to the Sunday bands, as to the whole Salvation propaganda. They claimed the right of carrying on religious persecution, and they brought matters to such a pass that the original dispute was lost sight of, and the Salvationists, even when they did not attempt to play their instruments on Sunday, were exposed to ruffianly attacks . . . If the wishes of Eastbourne were to be ratified by Parliament there would be an end to religious freedom. Any sect which happened to be unpop-ular in a particular locality would be exposed to persecution and expulsion. Really, it is high time that the vast majority of the people of Eastbourne were taught the rudiments of common law as well as the decencies of common charity. Parliament cannot permit a little town in the corner of Sussex to arrogate to itself a right which is unknown to any other part of the country. The Salvationists are perfectly entitled to their processions on Sunday or weekday, and the Corporation of Eastbourne are not entitled to make by-laws which are hostile to the general legislation of the land . . . The Eastbourne authorities imagined they could abuse their powers by instituting a persecution against a propaganda which they dislike. They have now to learn that Parliament does not choose to tolerate a trumpery Torquemada in a Sussex watering place.*[55]

Perhaps not unsurprisingly, Admiral Field, M.P. for Eastbourne, took the lead in opposing the Bill. He said of his constituency,

It wishes to have no controversy, no trouble of this kind with the Salvation Army. And I desire to recognise all the good that it is doing and endeavouring to do, although I do not like the methods adopted in carrying out that work. But it is a lamentable thing that Mr Booth should insist upon defying the law and acting, as I venture to say, contrary to the faith which he is supposed to teach.[56]

A debate of some three hours then took place following which the Bill passed its Second Reading by 269:122 votes, a majority of 147. When the news was received by the Eastbourne Corps they were understandably delighted. A Salvation Army press release described their feelings as

[like] a soul full of new found joy, they felt it impossible they should keep it to themselves, and they hurried hither and thither to tell the anxious ones at home.[57]

The news was not received so happily by many in Eastbourne. The Watch Committee met the next day and agreed to oppose the Bill in its future stages. The Salvation Army wisely decided that they would not march with music on the following Sunday. The mob which had gathered outside the Citadel saw nothing and made their way off along Seaside Road where they were entertained by a Militia brass band which was actually marching to a nearby church.

At the Lords Select Committee, Mr Pember Q.C. put to their Lordships that altogether there were four reasons to repeal Clause 169. First, that it represented an alteration to Common Law in one location only, that it was directed against one group, that it had been invented and then used to suppress one form of religious propaganda and, finally, the clause had brought about disastrous breaches of the peace. The members of the Select Committee agreed and the Bill

both Houses without further division. The Eastbourne

Improvement (1885) Amendment Act was to come into law on 1 September 1892.

When Admiral Field got back to Eastbourne later that evening he told a waiting crowd they had only been defeated because a General Election was imminent. He also told them that although they had lost the vote a great moral victory had been won. Meanwhile, General Booth sent a letter to the Eastbourne Corps congratulating them on their success and encouraged them to be magnanimous in victory.

> *Your comrades throughout the world, who have eagerly read from week to week the story of your devotion, and who have prayed God for the grace and strength to enable you to persevere, are rejoicing in the tidings of victory which are now known to all, and will for years to come make the name of your town a watch-word and a stimulus in the defence of liberty to publish Christ and His Salvation to the sons of men. And now, what next? There must be no exultation from any party or selfish feeling: on these grounds let there not be even an unfriendly reference to the past. As far as possible let the very memory of it be buried in oblivion. Let it not be forgotten for a moment that we have not been striving for the mastery, or in any spirit of self-glorification, but solely for the liberty to spread the knowledge of that religion the essence of which is love, and the manifestation of which is only by deeds of mercy, making known the life and work of the Christ who came to save . . . [58]*

The Bill came before a Hybrid Committee in early May. Mayor Morrison, Councillor Chambers, Chief Constable Fraser and others from Eastbourne Council were asked to be present. Members of the Salvation Army Corps in Eastbourne were also invited as was General Booth, by now an old man, who came to Parliament with his ear trumpet. The Salvation Army was again represented by Mr Pember Q.C. who outlined for the committee what had gone on in Eastbourne as a result of Clause 169.

The result of that Law had been that men and women have
been sent wholesale to prison; there had been riots and assaults,
most of them upon women, and throughout the whole of
proceedings the conduct of the police in enforcing the law had
been exceedingly rough. He contended that no Corporation had
a right to say "We dislike the Salvation Army so much that
we are entitled to have the common law of England altered in
that regard."[59]

When Mayor Morrison appeared before the Committee he
was pointedly asked about a number of comments he had
made regarding the Salvation Army. The Mayor said that his
comment about wanting to join the Skeleton Army had been
just a joke. When asked to reflect on his description of
Salvationists as "animals with two legs" he suggested it was
"rather poetical". As Mayor and chief magistrate in the town
these two comments were, of course, somewhat injudicious
but it was another which was especially telling in the circumstances. During a police court trial Mayor Morrison had
described the Salvation Army as " . . . an atrocious, infamous,
and degrading movement." When asked to defend this
comment the Mayor pointed out that he was not sitting on
the bench that day. He was again asked if this was another
joke to which he replied that " . . . it was said with all faith".
The Committee put it to him that perhaps these were not the
remarks to be made by a mayor of the town to whom his
fellow citizens would look to support law and order, to which
he replied, "It was in support of law and order."

Councillor Chambers was also appeared before the
Committee. In answer to questions the Councillor confirmed
that he had written to a local newspaper in May 1891 in which
he had suggested, "The Salvation Army is a body which is
built up with hypocrisy on a foundation of humbug,
cemented by false pretences." He also admitted that while at
a public meeting he had said, "For his own part he believed
the people of England were beginning to judge this Booth

movement was an organised hypocrisy." Mr Pember put to the Committee that on the basis of the evidence heard from the two men the disturbances in Eastbourne were clearly prompted by a dislike of the Salvation Army. The Committee members took the point and duly passed the Bill on a majority vote.

In June the Bill proceeded to come before a Select Committee of the House of Lords. Members took a particular interest in the process by which Clause 169 had entered the legislation. The evidence which came before their Lordships was most significant. Mr Adams, a member of the Eastbourne Council Law and Parliamentary Committee which had originally dealt with the Improvement Bill in 1884 was asked whether he or anyone else had had knowledge of the clause in the Bill. He denied this and added that the clause had not been in the manuscript draft of the Bill. Mr Adams even said that when the clause had come before the Council Meeting it was rejected and several members had left at that point only for those who remained to reinsert it. Councillor Reuben Climpson confirmed that an irregularity had taken place in that the clause was not included in the draft when put before the Council. Mr Pember, again representing the Salvation Army, took opportunity to remind their Lordships how the Bill had passed through the Commons at this time. The House Police and Sanitary Regulations Committee which dealt with all Improvement Bills usually comprised nine or ten members at the very least but, on this occasion, had only four present. This fact was not told to the House nor were members alerted through the Committee's report to Clause 169 which was a substantive matter being a change to common law. Mr Pember said that, in effect, members had voted in the dark. The Committee heard how Clause 169 was not only contrary to common law but it had been a major contributory factor in the Eastbourne disturbances.

Witnesses also gave evidence of the apparent bias against the Salvation Army on the part of the Council. It was said that whereas the clause was used to prohibit the Salvationist band from playing on Sunday, this did not extend to other bands. The Militia, Volunteer and Naval Reserve bands played on certain Sundays and no complaint was ever made against them. Witnesses said that many people in Eastbourne actually liked to hear bands playing on Sundays and, at times, a band could attract several thousand to listen. When the Volunteer manoeuvres had taken place locally there had been as many as twenty bands playing on Sunday. Again, there had been no complaints. The witnesses suggested to the Committee that it was not brass bands playing on Sunday to which people objected but, rather, those who played in them. In other words, their band was an excuse to focus opposition on the Salvation Army.

Though not required to come before the Committee, Walter Guy provides a personal account in describing an attack on a Salvation Army band which actually took place on a Thursday:

It became known one Thursday evening that the Army intended to go for a march. The roughs got to hear of it and said if we went they would kill us. We had heard that one before so did not take any notice of the threat and went just the same. It was a very dark night but fine, the crowd was a tremendous one and in a very desperate mood with lots of stuff to throw at us – of a very nasty nature. We went up Langney Road to Cavendish Place and round through to Seaside and round the Fountain back to the Citadel. The crowd were frantic when we got back and had got hold of lots of stones, brickends and the like. When the meeting had started they began to throw them through the windows, smashing everything they could, some were thrown so hard that they went through the windows and over the gallery right down onto the platform. They seemed as though they were mad and followed these up by throwing some very, very ripe eggs into the building. It got so bad that the people rushed out of the building and they were met with more eggs at close range. The stench was fearful, there was no fresh air anywhere and they did not know where to go. I think it was the worst experience of that sort we had during the whole period.[60]

The issue of the treatment given to Salvationist women was also considered. Their Lordships heard how women were targeted by the mobs not only for physical attacks but also sexual abuse, as well as extremely foul language. In her evidence Emily Mills told how she had been beaten and sexually abused by a mob of about forty men who laughed and jeered at her pain and humiliation. She had consequently felt ashamed and unable to disclose to the police what had happened. To add to her suffering Emily Mills told how she had been sacked by her employer for attending Parliament that day to give evidence. Several other women gave similar accounts of their mistreatment at the hands of the mob.

When those opposed to the repeal Bill gave their evidence before the Committee that given by the Mayor is especially noteworthy. Mayor Morrison put it that he had always tried hard to protect the Salvation Army in Eastbourne and had worked tirelessly to do so. There were only two Sundays when he had not attended their processions and that was on account of illness. He denied any hostility towards the Salvation Army. The Mayor was pressed with a question about a comment made in a speech made in November 1891 at a meeting of the local Volunteer force when he had said:

. . . the Volunteers of Eastbourne would make as good an example of any invading Army as the people of Eastbourne had made of another Army.[61]

Mayor Morrison was then asked to reflect on another comment he had made and about which he had earlier been asked by the Commons Hybrid Committee. He was again asked how he now felt having described the Salvation Army

as " . . . an atrocious, infamous and degrading movement".
He answered that he stuck by every word.

In summing up the Council's opposition to the repeal Bill
Mr Littler told the Committee:

> *Here are professing Christians deliberately breaking the law;*
> *the roughs see the police going to prevent them, and they aid*
> *the police . . . even the tambourine girls shook their tambourines*
> *in the faces of the mob. What can be imagined worse than that?*
> *I say again that even now, notwithstanding all the provocation*
> *that there has been on the part of these people, there is not the*
> *slightest desire on the part of the authorities to harass them.*[62]

When Mr Pember summed up in support of the Bill he put
something of a different case, asking the members to consider
that

> *. . . dislike is not a proper ground for legislation . . . When*
> *dislike crystallises into a clause in a statute it become legislative*
> *persecution, and in this case it becomes persecution of the worst*
> *kind – religious persecution.*[63]

After withdrawing to consider their response the Committee
returned to say that the Bill should proceed.

When the Council met in the Autumn they were forced
to consider their next move in the radically changed circumstances. Their own Finance Committee reported that
between May 1891 and September 1892 the expenditure on
the Salvation Army disturbances had been some £2000, set
against a Borough Rate of not quite £6000. Notwithstanding
this degree of expenditure the Council determined to press
on. At first, an appeal was made to the House of Lords but
this came to nothing. In response, an application was then
made to the Home Secretary for a byelaw but as this was
almost identical to the previous legislation he denied their
application.

For the next few months the Salvation Army maintained something of a low profile in the town. Taking the longer view, they had decided not to do anything which might damage local relations following the repeal of Clause 169. By early in the New Year their Sunday processions were attracting only 200 people with no reports of violence but only some jeering at the marchers. In the Summer there was further encouragement when the Salvation Army Brass Band accepted an invitation to join church choirs and musicians in a grand procession around the town in celebration of the wedding of Prince George, Duke of York, and Princess Mary of Teck. The procession also included several of the Councillors who had opposed the Army with such determination.

It was at this time that Mayor Morrison took the decision to retire from public office. He continued to enjoy a great popularity in Eastbourne but his health was by now broken. The Mayor had suffered badly with the strain and anxiety of his duties during the disturbances. Sleepless nights and a protracted and active involvement during the day meant he was exhausted. Mayor Morrison died suddenly in December 1895, aged only 52. When the news broke prayers were offered at the Citadel and it was agreed unanimously to write a letter of sympathy to Mrs Morrison and the family. The funeral at St Saviour's was attended by a huge congregation which included many dignitaries drawn from the many areas of life in which the Mayor had been involved. The congregation also included men and women from the Eastbourne Corps of the Salvation Army.

With regard to Mayor Morrison perhaps some words spoken before the Select Committee of the House of Lords by Mr Pember Q.C. offer an interesting perspective?

Against his character I desire to say absolutely nothing. He is a gentleman whom I have the honour of knowing to deserve all that I should desire to say in his favour in every respect except for the erroneous views which he has taken up, and the erroneous conduct, I venture to think, which he has undertaken and displayed with regard to the Salvation Army.[64]

In the following years a spirit of reconciliation and renewal blossomed in Eastbourne. In 1896, on the occasion of a bazaar at the Citadel, visitors cannot have failed to notice a large banner hung above the platform which read 'God bless the Mayor'. Indeed, the new Mayor, Alderman J.A. Skinner, was present together with other Council Members and all were warmly welcomed. When the Mayor rose to speak to those present he said:

There was a little difference of opinion among some as to whether he was doing his duty in going there . . . but he believed himself to be the servant of every section of the town, and he believed it to be his duty as Mayor to be here that afternoon . . . To him it made not the slightest difference whether it was the Salvation Army or the Church of England, or any other denomination . . . There was no need for him to say much. What was our life? We were anxious to do all we could for our fellow creatures. He hoped that as we passed through life we should always endeavour to help others.[65]

Though he had at first been against Sunday bands, Alderman Strange spoke in a similar vein. He told people

It was true that he hadn't got the red jacket, but he was just as much a soldier for all that, though belonging to another battalion . . . They were all on the side of right; they were all striving to make the world better, and for that reason were deserving of all support.[66]

By way of a reply, Major Emerson proposed a hearty vote of thanks to the Mayor and all the other Councillors with him, adding,

The presence of the Mayor that day had cheered them very much. His Worship could safely reckon that the Salvation Army would remain faithful citizens of bonny Eastbourne.[67]

As Mayor Skinner left the Citadel he was played out by the Salvation Army brass band.

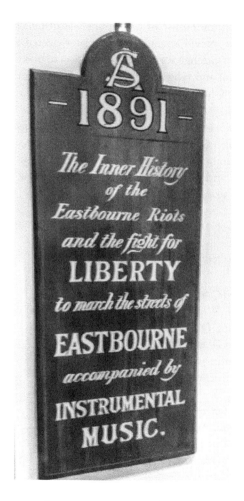

Commemorative Wall Plaque

1   *Eastbourne Gazette*, 16 May 1883.
2   *Eastbourne Gazette*, 22 August 1883.
3   *Eastbourne Gazette*, 2 January 1884.
4   *Eastbourne Gazette*, 27 August 1884.
5   *Eastbourne Gazette*, 24 September 1884.
6   *Eastbourne Gazette*, 1 October 1884.
7   *Eastbourne Gazette*, 8 October 1884.
8   *Eastbourne Gazette*, 4 November 1891.
9   The Eastbourne House of Commons was originally the idea of a local draper, Nevill Strange who was later elected as Alderman on the Council. Strange wanted his innovation to make a contribution to the moral and religious well-being of the town. According to Councillor Chambers the Eastbourne House of Commons was to be *an ordinary Debating Society to discuss the current topics of the day . . . the dominant idea was to make the new Society a reflex of the House of Commons.* Chambers (1910), *Eastbourne Memories*, Sumfield, p. 93. Chambers, in fact, played a leading role in the House of Commons and was elected as the first Speaker, an office he held for several years. Mr Strange was Prime Minister.
10 *Eastbourne Gazette*, 10 December 1884.
11 *All the World*, March 1892.
12 *Ibid.*
13 *Hansard*, 10 March 1892.
14 *Ibid.*
15 *All the World, op. cit.*
16 Quoted in Wiggins (1964), *The History of the Salvation Army, Volume Four, 1886–1904*, Thomas Nelson, p. 269.
17 *Eastbourne Gazette*, 4 June 1890.
18 See Appendix.
19 *Eastbourne Gazette*, 17 September 1890.
20 *Ibid.*
21 *Eastbourne Gazette*, 22 October 1890.
22 *All the World*, August 1891.
23 *Eastbourne Gazette*, 13 May 1891.
24 *Eastbourne Gazette*, 23 May 1891.
25 *Ibid.*
26 Guy (1964), *Marching with Music*, Eastbourne Citadel Corps, p. 6.
27 Guy, *op. cit.*, p. 2.
28 *Eastbourne Gazette*, 3 June 1891.
29 *Ibid.*

30 Guy, *op. cit.*, p.9.

31 *Eastbourne Gazette*, 1 July 1891.

32 *Ibid.*

33 Chambers, *op. cit.*, p. 210.

34 Guy, *op. cit.*, p. 12.

35 *The War Cry*, 25 July 1891.

36 *Eastbourne Gazette*, 22 July 1891.

37 *Ibid.*

38 *Ibid.*

39 Guy, *op. cit.*, p. 10.

40 Newspaper reports from outside Eastbourne throw some light on proceedings. *The Western Daily Press*, 20 July 1891, stated that the nine men were arrested on the responsibility of the Mayor and the Watch Committee while *The Western Times,* 21 July 1891, added some clarity by saying that the later telegram stated that the arrest was made on the responsibility of the Mayor and Watch Committee and not, as reported elsewhere, on the advice of the Home Secretary. At the trial of the bandsmen the Prosecution told the court that the Mayor, himself, gave instructions to the police to prevent a breach of the peace in a public street. This point was confirmed by the Chief Constable who said that he had taken the band into custody on the instructions of the Mayor. In his memoirs, Mr Fovargue, the Town Clerk at the time, recollected that the arrest of the nine bandsmen was by order of the Mayor. Fovargue (1933), *Municipal Eastbourne: Selections from the Proceedings of the Town Council*, Eastbourne C.B.C., p. 13.

41 *Eastbourne Gazette*, 22 July 1891.

42 *Ibid.*

43 *Eastbourne Gazette*, 9 September 1891.

44 Quoted in Walker (2001), *Pulling the Devil's Kingdom Down*, University of California Press, pp. 231–2.

45 *Eastbourne Gazette*, 16 September 1891.

46 *Eastbourne Gazette*, 7 October 1891.

47 *Eastbourne Gazette*, 4 November 1891.

48 *Ibid.*

49 *Ibid.*

50 *Ibid.*

51 Quoted in Wiggins, *op. cit.*, p. 274.

52 Quoted in Bovey (2015), *Blood on the Flag*, Shield Books, p. 356.

53 *Eastbourne Gazette*, 30 January 1892.

54 Quoted in Bovey, *op. cit.*, p. 359.

55 *Eastbourne Gazette*, 12 March 1892.

56 Quoted in Bovey, *op. cit.*, p. 359.

57 Salvation Army International Headquarters Eastbourne *The Conquering Hero Was Not Needed*, Press Release.

58 Quoted In Wiggins, *op. cit.*, p. 278.

59 *Eastbourne Gazette*, 30 April 1892.

60 Guy, *op. cit.*, p. 11.

61 Minutes of Evidence taken before the Select Committee of the House of Lords on the Eastbourne Improvement Act, 1885, Amendment Bill, 21 June 1892.

62 Minutes of Speech taken before the Select Committee of the House of Lords on the Eastbourne Improvement Act, 1885, Amendment Bill, 21 June 1892.

63 Minutes of Speech taken before the Select Committee of the House of Lords on the Eastbourne Improvement Act, 1885, Amendment Bill, 17 June 1892.

64 *Ibid.*

65 *Eastbourne Gazette*, 3 June 1896.

66 *Ibid.*

67 *Ibid.*

APPENDIX

This poem appeared in the *Eastbourne Gazette*, 11 June 1890.

The Deluge: or the Alderman, the Hose, and the "The Army"

A most heartrending story I have to relate
Concerning a flood, which, remorseless as fate,
Submerged part of Eastbourne and swept to the sea
The whole local corps of the Salvation Armee!

One fine Sunday morning about 10 o'clock
The big drum was beaten how grievous the shock
To the nerves of "old women" who now represent
The town in the Council when money is spent.

But Alderman T., who was dauntless and brave
Cried out to the Army "Attention I crave".
If you invade Sussex Gardens, I solemnly swear
I will turn the hose on you, so there and so there.

Alas for the Army they marched straight ahead,
Soldiers shouted, and sang, and waved banners so red,
And the Alderman proving as good as his word,
A sound as the roar of Niag'ra was heard.

The water gushed forth in a furious stream,
The Salvation sisters gave a loud and shrill scream,
And borne from the earth and immersed in the flood,
Were soldiers with vestments inscribed "Fire and Blood".

In pell mell confusion they were all whirled along,
And ended for aye was their ear-splitting song!
The big drum soon floated alone on the wave,
While the soloist gurgled "O save me! O save".

The Army was swept away by the tide,
Which bore them away to the ocean so wide.
What more remains for me to add about the rushing water?
It swept away the whole East End !
O dire and dismal slaughter!

BIBLIOGRAPHY

August (2007), *The British Working Class 1832–1940*, Pearson Longman.

Booth (1890), *In Darkest England, and the Way Out*, Funk & Wagnalls.

Bailey, *Salvation Army Riots, the 'Skeleton Army' and Legal Authority in the Provincial Town*, in Donajgrodzki (1977), *Social Control in Nineteenth Century Britain*, Croom Helm.

Bovey (2015), *Blood on the Flag*, Shield Books.

Briggs, *The Salvation Army in Sussex* in Kitch (ed.) (1981), *Studies in Sussex Church History*, Leopard's Head Press.

Chambers (1910), *East Bourne Memories of the Victorian Period, 1845–1901*, Sumfield.

Fovargue (1933), *Municipal Eastbourne: Selections from the Proceedings of the Town Council*, Eastbourne C.B.C.

Graham (1888), *Eastbourne Recollections*, Hollaway.

Griggs (2016), *Eastbourne 1851–1951 – A Social History*, Grosvenor House.

Guy (1964), *Marching with Music*, Eastbourne Citadel Corps.

Hare (1988), *The Skeleton Army and the Bonfire Boys, Worthing, 1884*, Folklore, Vol. 99: ii.

Hattersley (1999), *Blood and Fire*, Little, Brown and Company.

Holz (2006), *Brass Bands of the Salvation Army, Volume One, Their Mission and Music*, Streets Publishers.

Horridge (2015), *The Salvation Army Origins and Early Days: 1865–1900*, Abernant Publishing.

Inglis (1963), *Churches and the Working Classes in Victorian England*, Routledge and Kegan Paul.

Joy (1975), *The Old Corps*, Salvationist Publishing.

Kneale *The Battle of Torquay: The Late Victorian Resort as Social Experiment*, in Ingleby, Matthew and Kerr (eds.) (2018), *Coastal Cultures of the Long Nineteenth Century*, University of Edinburgh Press.

Longmate (1968), *The Water-Drinkers*, Hamish Hamilton.

Mayhew (2008), *London Labour and the London Poor*, Wordsworth.

McLeod (1974), *Class and Religion in the Late Victorian City*, Croom Helm.

McLeod (1984), *Religion and the Working Class in Nineteenth-Century Britain*, Macmillan.

Murdoch (1992), Salvation Army Disturbances in Liverpool, England, 1879–1882, in *Journal of Social History*, Volume 25, Issue 3.

Murdoch (1994), *Origins of the Salvation Army*, The University of Tennessee Press.

Neville (1982), *Religion and Society in Eastbourne 1735–1920*, Eastbourne Local History Society.

Railton (1889), *Twenty one years' Salvation Army: Under the generalship of William Booth*, The Salvation Army Publishing Offices.

Sandall (1947), *The History of the Salvation Army, Volume One, 1865–1878*, Thomas Nelson and Sons.

Smith, *The Formation of the Eastbourne Police Force in 1891*.

Smith (1990), *The Whitchurch Salvation Army Disturbances 1881–1890*, Whitchurch Local History Society.

Stiles (1995), *Religion, Society and Reform 1800–1914*, Hodder & Stoughton.

Vickers (1989), *The Religious Census of Sussex*, Sussex Record Society.

Vorspan (1997), *Freedom of Assembly and the Right to Passage in Modern English Legal History*, Fordham Law School.

Walker (2001), *Pulling the Devil's Kingdom Down*, University of California Press.

Wiggins (1964), *The History of the Salvation Army, Volume Four*, Thomas Nelson.

Wigley (1980), *The Rise and Fall of the Victorian Sunday*, Manchester University Press.

Journals

The East London Evangelist, October 1868.

The Palace Journal, 24 April 1889.

All the World, August 1891.

All the World, October 1891.

All the World, January 1892.

All the World, February 1892.

All the World, March 1892.

All the World, July 1892.

The War Cry, 25 July 1891.
The War Cry, 18 January 1964.

Eastbourne Council papers

Minutes of Council, October 1888–October 1892.
Minutes of Watch Committee, November 1890–June 1892.

Parliamentary papers

Hansard, 10 March 1892.
Minutes of Evidence taken before the Select Committee of the House of Lords on the Eastbourne Improvement Act, 1885, Amendment Bill, 17 June 1892.
Minutes of Speech taken before the Select Committee of the House of Lords on the Eastbourne Improvement Act, 1885, Amendment Bill, 17 June 1892.
Minutes of Evidence taken before the Select Committee of the House of Lords on the Eastbourne Improvement Act, 1885, Amendment Bill, 21 June 1892.
Minutes of Speech taken before the Select Committee of the House of Lords on the Eastbourne Improvement Act, 1885, Amendment Bill, 21 June 1892.

Websites

bbc.co.uk/history/british/victorians/seaside
britishnewspaperarchive.co.uk
en.wikipedia.org/wiki/Charivari
oldpolicecellsmuseum.org.uk
visiteastbourne.com/Eastbourne-Leaf-Hall-History-Corner

INDEX

Printed and bound by CPI Group (UK) Ltd, Croydon, CR0 4YY